Creole Ambrosia

A refreshing cold fruity pudding that can be made at any time of the year.

INGREDIENTS

Serves 6

6 oranges

1 coconut

25g/1oz/2 tbsp caster sugar

1 Peel the oranges removing all white pith, then slice thinly, picking out seeds with the point of a knife. Do this on a plate to catch the juice.

2 Pierce the "eyes" of the coconut and pour away the milk, then crack open the coconut with a hammer. (This is best done outside on a stone surface.)

> ## COOK'S TIP
> Mangoes instead of oranges make the dessert more exotic but less authentically Creole.

3 Peel the coconut with a sharp knife, then grate half the flesh coarsely, either on a hand grater or on the grating blade of a blender or food processor.

4 Layer the coconut and orange slices in a glass bowl, starting and finishing with the coconut. After each orange layer, sprinkle on a little sugar and pour over some of the reserved orange juice.

5 Let the dessert stand for 2 hours before serving, either at room temperature or, in hot weather, keep it refrigerated.

Watermelon Sherbet

*A pretty pink sherbet that makes a
light and refreshing dessert, or that
could be served before the main
course to cleanse the palate at a
grand dinner.*

INGREDIENTS

Serves 6

1kg/2¼lb piece watermelon

200g/7oz/1 cup caster sugar

juice of 1 lemon

2 egg whites

mint leaves, to decorate

1 Cut the watermelon in wedges,
then cut it away from the rind,
cubing the flesh and picking out all
the seeds.

2 Purée three-quarters of the
flesh in a food processor or
blender, but mash the last quarter
on a plate – this will give the
sherbet more texture.

3 Stir the sugar with the lemon
juice and 120ml/4fl oz/½ cup
cold water in a saucepan over very
low heat until the sugar dissolves
and the syrup clears.

4 Mix all the watermelon and
the syrup in a large bowl and
transfer to a freezer container.

5 Freeze for 1–1½ hours, until
the edges begin to set. Beat the
mixture, return to the freezer and
freeze for a further 1 hour.

6 When the hour is up, whisk the
egg whites to soft peaks. Beat
the iced mixture again and fold in
the egg whites. Return to the
freezer for a further 1 hour, then
beat once more and freeze firm.

7 Transfer the sherbet from
the freezer to the fridge for
20–30 minutes before it is to be
served. Serve in scoops, decorated
with mint leaves.

Coffee, Vanilla and Chocolate Stripe

This looks really special served in elegant wine glasses and tastes appropriately exquisite.

INGREDIENTS

Serves 6

285g/10½oz/1½ cups caster sugar
90ml/6 tbsp cornflour
900ml/1½ pints/3¾ cups milk
3 egg yolks
75g/3oz/6 tbsp unsalted butter, at room
    temperature
20ml/generous 1 tbsp instant coffee
    powder
10ml/2 tsp vanilla essence
30ml/2 tbsp cocoa powder
whipped cream, to serve

1 To make the coffee layer, place 90g/3½oz/½ cup of the sugar and 30ml/2 tbsp of the cornflour in a heavy-based saucepan. Gradually add one-third of the milk, whisking until well blended. Over a medium heat, whisk in one of the egg yolks and bring to the boil, whisking. Boil for 1 minute.

2 Remove the pan from the heat. Stir in 25g/1oz/2 tbsp of the butter and the instant coffee powder. Set aside in the pan to cool slightly.

3 Divide the coffee mixture among six wine glasses. Smooth the tops before the mixture sets.

4 Wipe any dribbles on the insides and outsides of the glasses with damp kitchen paper.

5 To make the vanilla layer, place half of the remaining sugar and cornflour in a heavy-based saucepan. Whisk in 300ml/ ½ pint/1¼ cups of the milk. Over a medium heat, whisk in another egg yolk and bring to the boil, whisking. Boil for 1 minute.

6 Remove the pan from the heat and stir in 25g/1oz/2 tbsp of the butter and the vanilla. Leave to cool slightly, then spoon into the glasses on top of the coffee layer. Smooth the tops and wipe the glasses with kitchen paper.

7 To make the chocolate layer, place the remaining sugar and cornflour in a heavy-based saucepan. Gradually whisk in the remaining milk and continue whisking until blended. Over a medium heat, whisk in the last egg yolk and bring to the boil, whisking constantly. Boil for 1 minute. Remove from the heat, stir in the remaining butter and the cocoa. Leave to cool slightly, then spoon into the glasses on top of the vanilla layer. Chill until set.

8 Pipe swirls of whipped cream on top of each dessert just before serving.

COOK'S TIP

For a special occasion, prepare the vanilla layer using a fresh vanilla pod. Choose a plump, supple pod and split it down the centre with a sharp knife. Add to the mixture with the milk and discard the pod before spooning the mixture into the glasses. The flavour will be more pronounced and the pudding will have pretty brown speckles from the vanilla seeds.

Chocolate Hazelnut Galettes

Chocolate rounds sandwiched with fromage frais. If only all sandwiches looked and tasted this good.

INGREDIENTS

Serves 4

175g/6oz plain chocolate, broken into
    squares
45ml/3 tbsp single cream
30ml/2 tbsp flaked hazelnuts
115g/4oz white chocolate, broken into
    squares
175g/6oz/¾ cup fromage frais (8% fat)
15ml/1 tbsp dry sherry
60ml/4 tbsp finely chopped hazelnuts,
    toasted
physalis (Cape gooseberries), dipped in
    white chocolate, to decorate

1 Melt the plain chocolate in a heatproof bowl over hot water, then remove from the heat and stir in the cream.

2 Draw 12 x 7.5cm/3in circles on sheets of non-stick baking paper. Turn the paper over and spread the plain chocolate over each marked circle, covering in a thin, even layer. Scatter flaked hazelnuts over four of the circles, then leave to set.

3 Melt the white chocolate in a heatproof bowl over hot water, then stir in the fromage frais and dry sherry. Fold in the chopped, toasted hazelnuts. Leave to cool until the mixture holds its shape.

4 Remove the chocolate rounds carefully from the paper and sandwich them together in stacks of three, spooning the hazelnut cream between each layer and using the hazelnut-covered rounds on top. Chill before serving.

5 To serve, place the galettes on individual plates and decorate with chocolate-dipped physalis.

COOK'S TIP

The chocolate could be spread over heart shapes instead, for a special Valentine's Day dessert.

Chocolate and Chestnut Pots

Prepared in advance, these are the
perfect ending for a dinner party.
Remove them from the fridge about
30 minutes before serving, to allow
them to "ripen".

Serves 6

250g/9oz plain chocolate

60ml/4 tbsp Madeira

25g/1oz/2 tbsp butter, diced

2 eggs, separated

225g/8oz/scant 1 cup unsweetened
   chestnut purée

crème fraîche or whipped double cream,
   to decorate

1 Make a few chocolate curls for
decoration, then break the rest
of the chocolate into squares and
melt it with the Madeira in a
saucepan over a gentle heat.
Remove from the heat and add the
butter, a few pieces at a time,
stirring until melted and smooth.

COOK'S TIP

If Madeira is not available, use
brandy or rum instead. These
chocolate pots can be frozen
successfully for up to 2 months.

2 Beat the egg yolks quickly into
the mixture, then beat in the
chestnut purée, mixing until
smooth.

3 Whisk the egg whites in a
clean, grease-free bowl until
stiff. Stir about 15ml/1 tbsp of the
whites into the chestnut mixture to
lighten it, then fold in the rest
smoothly and evenly.

4 Spoon the mixture into six
small ramekin dishes and chill
until set. Serve the pots topped
with a generous spoonful of crème
fraîche or whipped double cream
and decorated with the plain
chocolate curls.

Coffee Ice Cream with Caramelized Pecans

Coffee and sweetened nuts make a mouth-watering combination.

INGREDIENTS

Serves 4–6

For the ice cream

300ml/10fl oz/1¼ cups milk
1 tbsp demerara sugar
25g/1oz/6 tbsp finely ground coffee or
   1 tbsp instant coffee granules
1 egg plus 2 yolks
300ml/10fl oz/1¼ cups double cream
1 tbsp caster sugar

For the pecans

115g/4oz/1 cup pecan halves
50g/2oz/4 tbsp soft dark brown sugar

1 Heat the milk and demerara sugar to boiling point. Remove from the heat and sprinkle on the coffee. Leave to stand for 2 minutes, then stir, cover and cool.

2 In a heatproof bowl, beat the egg and extra yolks until the mixture is thick and pale.

COOK'S TIP
∿

You can give good-quality bought ice cream a fillip with the same nutty garnish.

3 Strain the coffee mixture into a clean pan, heat to boiling point, then pour on to the eggs in a steady stream, beating hard all the time.

4 Set the bowl over a pan of gently simmering water and stir until it thickens. Cool, then chill in the fridge.

5 Whip the cream with the caster sugar. Fold it into the coffee custard and freeze in a covered container. Beat twice at hourly intervals, then leave to freeze firm.

6 To caramelize the nuts, preheat the oven to 180°C/350°F/Gas 4. Spread the nuts on a baking sheet in a single layer. Put them into the oven for 10–15 minutes to toast until they release their fragrance.

7 On the top of the stove, dissolve the brown sugar in 2 tbsp water in a heavy-based pan, shaking it about over a low heat until the sugar dissolves completely and the syrup clears.

8 When the syrup begins to bubble, tip in the toasted pecans and cook for a minute or two over a medium heat until the syrup coats and clings to the nuts.

9 Spread the nuts on a lightly oiled baking sheet, separating them with the tip of a knife, and leave to cool. Store when cold in an airtight tin if they are not to be eaten on the same day.

10 Transfer the ice cream from the freezer to the fridge 30 minutes before scooping it into portions and serving with caramelized pecans.

White Chocolate Parfait

Everything you could wish for in a dessert; white and dark chocolate in one mouth-watering slice.

INGREDIENTS

Serves 10

225g/8oz white chocolate, chopped
600ml/1 pint/2½ cups whipping cream
120ml/4fl oz/½ cup milk
10 egg yolks
15ml/1 tbsp caster sugar
25g/1oz/scant ½ cup desiccated coconut
120ml/4fl oz/½ cup canned sweetened
   coconut milk
150g/5oz/1¼ cups unsalted macadamia
   nuts

For the chocolate icing

225g/8oz plain chocolate
75g/3oz/6 tbsp butter
20ml/generous 1 tbsp golden syrup
175ml/6fl oz/¾ cup whipping cream
curls of fresh coconut, to decorate

1 Line the base and sides of a 1.4 litre/2⅓ pint/6 cup terrine mould (25 x 10cm/10 x 4in) with clear film.

2 Place the chopped white chocolate and 50ml/2fl oz/½ cup of the cream in the top of a double boiler or in a heatproof bowl set over hot water. Stir until melted and smooth. Set aside.

3 Put 250ml/8fl oz/1 cup of the cream and the milk in a pan and bring to boiling point.

4 Meanwhile, whisk the egg yolks and caster sugar together in a large bowl, until thick and pale.

5 Add the hot cream mixture to the yolks, beating constantly. Pour back into the saucepan and cook over a low heat for 2–3 minutes, until thickened. Stir constantly and do not boil. Remove the pan from the heat.

6 Add the melted chocolate, desiccated coconut and coconut milk, then stir well and leave to cool.

7 Whip the remaining cream until thick, then fold into the chocolate and coconut mixture.

8 Put 475ml/16fl oz/2 cups of the parfait mixture in the prepared mould and spread evenly. Cover and freeze for about 2 hours, until just firm. Cover the remaining mixture and chill.

9 Scatter the macadamia nuts evenly over the frozen parfait. Pour in the remaining parfait mixture. Cover the terrine and freeze for 6–8 hours or overnight, until the parfait is firm.

10 To make the icing, melt the chocolate with the butter and syrup in the top of a double boiler set over hot water. Stir occasionally.

11 Heat the cream in a saucepan, until just simmering, then stir into the chocolate mixture. Remove the pan from the heat and leave to cool until lukewarm.

12 To turn out the parfait, wrap the terrine in a hot towel and set it upside-down on a plate. Lift off the terrine mould, then peel off the clear film. Place the parfait on a rack over a baking sheet and pour the chocolate icing evenly over the top. Working quickly, smooth the icing down the sides with a palette knife. Leave to set slightly, then freeze for a further 3–4 hours. Cut into slices using a knife dipped in hot water. Serve, decorated with curls of fresh coconut.

White Chocolate Mousse with Dark Sauce

Creamy vanilla-flavoured white chocolate mousse is served with a dark rum and chocolate sauce.

INGREDIENTS

Serves 6–8

200g/7oz white chocolate, broken into
   squares
2 eggs, separated
60ml/4 tbsp caster sugar
300ml/½ pint/1¼ cups double cream
1 sachet powdered gelatine or alternative
150ml/¼ pint/⅔ cup Greek-style yogurt
10ml/2 tsp vanilla essence

For the sauce
50g/2oz plain chocolate, broken into
   squares
30ml/2 tbsp dark rum
60ml/4 tbsp single cream

1 Line a 1 litre/1¾ pint/4 cup loaf tin with non-stick baking paper or clear film. Melt the chocolate in a heatproof bowl over hot water, then remove from the heat.

2 Whisk the egg yolks and sugar in a bowl until pale and thick, then beat in the melted chocolate.

3 Heat the cream in a small saucepan until almost boiling, then remove from the heat. Sprinkle the powdered gelatine over, stirring gently until it is completely dissolved.

4 Then pour on to the chocolate mixture, whisking vigorously to mix until smooth.

5 Whisk the yogurt and vanilla essence into the mixture. In a clean, grease-free bowl, whisk the egg whites until stiff, then fold them into the mixture. Tip into the prepared loaf tin, level the surface and chill until set.

6 Make the sauce. Melt the chocolate with the rum and cream in a heatproof bowl over barely simmering water, stirring occasionally, then leave to cool.

7 When the mousse is set, remove it from the tin with the aid of the paper or clear film. Serve in thick slices with the cooled chocolate sauce poured around.

COOK'S TIP

Make sure the gelatine is completely dissolved in the cream before adding to the other ingredients.

Frozen Strawberry Mousse Cake

Children love this pretty dessert – it tastes just like an ice cream.

INGREDIENTS

Serves 4–6

425g/15oz can strawberries in syrup
15ml/1 tbsp/1 sachet powdered gelatine
6 trifle sponge cakes
45ml/3 tbsp strawberry jam
200ml/7fl oz/⅞ cup crème fraîche
200ml/7fl oz/⅞ cup whipped cream,
   to decorate

1 Strain the syrup from the strawberries into a large heatproof bowl. Sprinkle over the gelatine and stir well. Stand the bowl in a pan of hot water and stir until the gelatine has dissolved.

2 Leave to cool, then chill for just under 1 hour, until beginning to set. Meanwhile, cut the sponge cakes in half lengthways and spread the cut surfaces with the strawberry jam.

3 Carefully whisk the crème fraîche into the strawberry jelly, then whisk in the canned strawberries. Line a deep, 20cm/8in loose-based cake tin with non-stick baking paper.

4 Pour half the strawberry mousse mixture into the tin, arrange the sponge cakes over the surface, and then spoon over the remaining mousse mixture, pushing down any sponge cakes which rise up.

5 Freeze for 1–2 hours until firm. Remove the cake from the tin and carefully peel away the lining paper. Transfer to a serving plate. Decorate the mousse with whirls of whipped cream and a few strawberry leaves and a fresh strawberry, if you have them.

Iced Praline Torte

Make this elaborate torte several days ahead, decorate it and return it to the freezer until you are nearly ready to serve it. Allow the torte to stand at room temperature for an hour before serving, or leave it in the refrigerator overnight to soften.

INGREDIENTS

Serves 8

115g/4oz/1 cup almonds or hazelnuts
115g/4oz/8 tbsp caster sugar
115g/4oz/⅔ cup raisins
90ml/6 tbsp rum or brandy
115g/4oz dark chocolate, broken into
   squares
30ml/2 tbsp milk
450ml/¾ pint/1⅞ cups double cream
30ml/2 tbsp strong black coffee
16 sponge-finger biscuits

To finish
150ml/¼ pint/⅔ cup double cream
50g/2oz/½ cup flaked almonds, toasted
15g/½oz dark chocolate, melted

1 To make the praline, have ready an oiled cake tin or baking sheet. Put the nuts into a heavy-based pan with the sugar and heat gently until the sugar melts. Swirl the pan to coat the nuts in the hot sugar. Cook slowly until the nuts brown and the sugar caramelizes. Transfer the nuts quickly to the tin or tray and leave them to cool completely. Break them up and grind them to a fine powder in a blender or food processor.

2 Soak the raisins in 45ml/3 tbsp of the rum or brandy for an hour (or better still overnight), so they soften and absorb the rum. Melt the chocolate with the milk in a bowl over a pan of hot, but not boiling water. Remove and allow to cool. Lightly grease a 1.2 litre/ 2 pint/5 cup loaf tin and line it with greaseproof paper.

3 Whisk the cream in a bowl until it holds soft peaks. Whisk in the cold chocolate. Then fold in the praline and the soaked raisins, with any liquid.

4 Mix the coffee and remaining rum or brandy in a shallow dish. Dip in the sponge-fingers and arrange half in a layer over the base of the prepared loaf tin.

5 Cover with the chocolate mixture and add another layer of soaked sponge-fingers. Leave in the freezer overnight.

6 Whip the double cream for the topping. Dip the tin briefly into warm water to loosen it and turn the torte out on to a serving plate. Cover with the whipped cream, sprinkle the top with toasted flaked almonds and drizzle the melted chocolate over the top. Return the torte to the freezer until it is needed.

COOK'S TIP

Make the praline in advance and store it in an airtight jar until needed.

Blackcurrant Sorbet

Blackcurrants make a vibrant and intensely flavoured sorbet.

INGREDIENTS

Serves 4–6

90g/3½oz/½ cup caster sugar

500g/1¼lb blackcurrants

juice of ½ lemon

15ml/1 tbsp egg white

mint leaves, to decorate

1 In a small saucepan over a medium-high heat, bring the sugar and 120ml/4fl oz/½ cup of water to the boil, stirring until the sugar dissolves. Boil the syrup for 2 minutes, then remove the pan from the heat and set aside to cool.

2 Remove the blackcurrants from the stalks, by pulling them through the tines of a fork.

3 In a blender or food processor fitted with a metal blade, process the blackcurrants and lemon juice until smooth. Alternatively, chop the blackcurrants coarsely, then add the lemon juice. Mix in the sugar syrup.

4 Press the purée through a sieve to remove the seeds.

5 Pour the blackcurrant purée into a non-metallic, freezer-proof dish. Cover the dish with clear film or a lid and freeze until the sorbet is nearly firm, but still a bit slushy.

6 Cut the sorbet into pieces and put into the blender or food processor. Process until smooth, then with the machine running, add the egg white and process until well mixed. Tip the sorbet back into the dish and freeze until almost firm. Chop the sorbet again and process until smooth.

7 Serve immediately or freeze, tightly covered, for up to 1 week. Allow to soften for 5–10 minutes at room temperature before serving, decorated with mint leaves.

Chocolate Ice Cream

Use good quality plain or cooking chocolate for the best flavour.

Makes about 850ml/1½ pints/3¾ cups

750ml/1¼ pints/3 cups milk

10cm/4in piece of vanilla pod

4 egg yolks

225g/8oz cooking chocolate, melted

150g/5oz/¾ cup granulated sugar

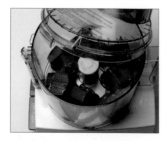

1 To make the custard, heat the milk with the vanilla pod in a small saucepan. Remove from the heat as soon as small bubbles start to form. Do not boil.

2 Beat the egg yolks with a wire whisk or electric beater. Gradually incorporate the sugar, and continue beating for about 5 minutes until the mixture is pale yellow. Strain the milk. Slowly add it to the egg mixture drop by drop.

3 Pour the mixture into a double boiler with the melted chocolate. Stir over moderate heat until the water in the pan is boiling, and the custard thickens enough to lightly coat the back of a spoon. Remove from the heat and allow to cool.

4 Freeze in an ice cream maker, or if you do not have an ice cream maker, pour the mixture into a metal or plastic freezer container and freeze until set, about 3 hours. Remove from the container and chop roughly into 7.5cm/3in pieces. Place in the bowl of a food processor and process until smooth. Return to the freezer container, and freeze again until firm. Repeat the freezing-chopping process 2 or 3 times, until a smooth consistency is reached.

Frozen Grand Marnier Soufflés

These sophisticated little puddings are always appreciated and make a wonderful end to a meal.

INGREDIENTS

Serves 8

200g/7oz/1 cup caster sugar
6 large eggs, separated
250ml/8fl oz/1 cup milk
15g/½oz powdered gelatine, soaked in
    45ml/3 tbsp cold water
450ml/¾ pint/1⅞ cups double cream
60ml/4 tbsp Grand Marnier

1 Tie a double-collar of grease-proof paper around eight ramekin dishes. Put 75g/3oz/6 tbsp of the sugar in a bowl with the egg yolks and whisk until pale.

2 Heat the milk until almost boiling and pour it on to the yolks, whisking all the time. Return to the pan and stir it over a gentle heat until it is thick enough to coat the spoon. Remove the pan from the heat and stir in the soaked gelatine. Pour into a bowl and leave to cool. Whisk occasionally, until it is on the point of setting.

3 Put the remaining sugar in a pan with 45ml/3 tbsp of water and dissolve it over a low heat. Bring to the boil and boil rapidly until it reaches the soft ball stage or 119°C/238°F on a sugar thermometer. Remove from the heat. In a clean bowl, whisk the egg whites until they are stiff. Pour the hot syrup on to the whites, whisking all the time. Set aside and leave to cool.

4 Whisk the cream until it holds soft peaks. Add the Grand Marnier to the cold custard and fold the custard into the cold meringue, with the cream. Quickly pour into the prepared ramekin dishes. Freeze overnight. Remove the paper collars. Leave the soufflés at room temperature for 30 minutes before serving.

Double Chocolate Snowball

This is an ideal party dessert as it can be prepared at least one day ahead and decorated on the day.

INGREDIENTS

Serves 12–14

350g/12oz plain chocolate, chopped
285g/10½oz/1½ cups caster sugar
275g/10oz/1¼ cups unsalted butter, cut
   into small pieces
8 eggs
50ml/2fl oz/¼ cup orange-flavoured
   liqueur or brandy (optional)
cocoa for dusting

For the white chocolate cream
200g/7oz fine quality white chocolate,
   broken into pieces
475ml/16fl oz/2 cups double or whipping
   cream
30ml/2 tbsp orange-flavour liqueur
   (optional)

1 Preheat the oven to 180°C/
350°F/Gas 4. Line a 1.75 litre/
3 pint/1½ quart round ovenproof
bowl with aluminium foil,
smoothing the sides. In a bowl
over a pan of simmering water,
melt the plain chocolate. Add the
sugar and stir until it dissolves.
Strain into a medium bowl. With
an electric mixer at low speed, beat
in the butter, then the eggs, one at
a time, beating well after each
addition. Stir in the liqueur or
brandy, if using, and pour into the
prepared bowl. Tap gently to
release any large air bubbles.

2 Bake for 1¼–1½ hours until
the surface is firm and slightly
risen, but cracked. The centre will
still be wobbly: this will set on
cooling. Remove to a rack to cool
to room temperature. Cover with a
plate, then cover completely with
clear film or foil and chill
overnight. To unmould, remove
plate and film or foil and invert
mould on to a plate; shake firmly
to release. Peel off foil. Cover until
ready to decorate.

3 Process the white chocolate in
a blender or food processor
until fine crumbs form. In a small
saucepan, heat 120ml/4fl oz/½ cup
of the cream until just beginning
to simmer. With the food
processor running, pour cream
through the feed tube and process
until the chocolate is completely
melted. Strain into a medium bowl
and cool to room temperature,
stirring occasionally.

4 Beat the remaining cream
until soft peaks form, add
the liqueur, if using, and beat for
30 seconds or until the cream just
holds its shape. Fold a spoonful of
cream into the chocolate then fold
in remaining cream. Spoon into
an icing bag fitted with a star tip
and pipe rosettes over the surface.
If you wish, dust with cocoa.

HOT
PUDDINGS

Hot Chocolate Zabaglione

A deliciously chocolate-flavoured variation of a classic Italian dessert.

INGREDIENTS

Serves 6

6 egg yolks

150g/5oz/¾ cup caster sugar

45ml/3 tbsp cocoa powder

200ml/7fl oz/⅞ cup Marsala

cocoa powder or icing sugar, for dusting

almond biscuits, to serve

1 Half fill a medium saucepan with water and bring to simmering point.

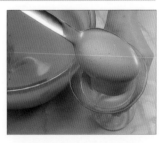

2 Place the egg yolks and sugar in a heatproof bowl and whisk until the mixture is pale and all the sugar has dissolved.

3 Add the cocoa and Marsala, then place the bowl over the simmering water. Whisk until the consistency of the mixture is smooth, thick and foamy.

4 Pour quickly into tall heatproof glasses, dust lightly with cocoa or icing sugar and serve immediately with almond biscuits.

Chocolate and Orange Scotch Pancakes

Fabulous baby pancakes in a rich creamy orange liqueur sauce.

INGREDIENTS

Serves 4

115g/4oz/1 cup self-raising flour

30ml/2 tbsp cocoa powder

2 eggs

50g/2oz plain chocolate, broken into
    squares

200ml/7fl oz/⅞ cup milk

finely grated rind of 1 orange

30ml/2 tbsp orange juice

butter or oil for frying

60ml/4 tbsp chocolate curls, for sprinkling

For the sauce

2 large oranges

30ml/2 tbsp unsalted butter

45ml/3 tbsp light muscovado sugar

250ml/8fl oz/1 cup crème fraîche

30ml/2 tbsp Grand Marnier or Cointreau

chocolate curls, to decorate

1 Sift the flour and cocoa into a bowl and make a well in the centre. Add the eggs and beat well, gradually incorporating the surrounding dry ingredients to make a smooth batter.

2 Mix the chocolate and milk in a saucepan. Heat gently until the chocolate has melted, then beat into the batter until smooth and bubbly. Stir in the grated orange rind and juice.

3 Heat a large heavy-based frying pan or griddle. Grease with a little butter or oil. Drop large spoonfuls of batter on to the hot surface. Cook over a moderate heat. When the pancakes are lightly browned underneath and bubbly on top, flip them over to cook the other side. Slide on to a plate and keep hot, then make more in the same way.

4 Make the sauce. Grate the rind of 1 of the oranges into a bowl and set aside. Peel both oranges, taking care to remove all the pith, then slice the flesh fairly thinly.

5 Heat the butter and sugar in a wide, shallow pan over a low heat, stirring until the sugar dissolves. Stir in the crème fraîche and heat gently.

6 Add the pancakes and orange slices to the sauce, heat gently for 1–2 minutes, then spoon over the liqueur. Sprinkle with the reserved orange rind. Scatter over the chocolate curls and serve the pancakes at once.

Amaretto Soufflé

*A mouth-watering soufflé with more
than a hint of Amaretto liqueur.*

INGREDIENTS

Serves 6

6 amaretti biscuits, coarsely crushed
90ml/4 tbsp Amaretto liqueur
4 eggs, separated, plus 1 egg white
130g/3½oz/½ cup caster sugar
30ml/2 tbsp plain flour
250ml/8fl oz/1 cup milk
pinch of cream of tartar (if needed)
icing sugar, for dusting

1 Preheat the oven to 200°C/
400°F/Gas 6. Butter a 1.5 litre/
2½ pint/6¼ cup soufflé dish and
sprinkle it with a little of the
caster sugar.

2 Put the biscuits in a bowl.
Sprinkle them with 30ml/
2 tbsp of the Amaretto liqueur and
set aside.

3 In another bowl, carefully mix
together the 4 egg yolks, 30ml/
2 tbsp of the sugar and all of the
flour.

4 Heat the milk just to the boil
in a heavy saucepan. Gradually
add the hot milk to the egg
mixture, stirring.

5 Pour the mixture back into the
pan. Set over a low heat and
simmer gently for 3–4 minutes or
until thickened, stirring occasionally.

6 Add the remaining Amaretto
liqueur. Remove from the heat.

7 In a scrupulously clean, grease-
free bowl, whisk the 5 egg
whites until they will hold soft
peaks. (If not using a copper bowl,
add the cream of tartar as soon as
the whites are frothy.) Add the
remaining sugar and continue
whisking until stiff.

8 Add about one-quarter of the
whites to the liqueur mixture
and stir in with a rubber spatula.
Add the remaining whites and fold
in gently.

9 Spoon half of the mixture into
the prepared soufflé dish.
Cover with a layer of the moistened
amaretti biscuits, then spoon the
remaining soufflé mixture on top.

10 Bake for 20 minutes or
until the soufflé is risen and
lightly browned. Sprinkle with
sifted icing sugar and serve
immediately.

Hot Mocha Rum Soufflés

Serve these superb soufflés as soon as they are cooked for a fantastic finale to a dinner party.

INGREDIENTS

Serves 6

25g/1oz/2 tbsp unsalted butter, melted
65g/2½ oz/generous ½ cup cocoa powder
75g/3oz/generous ⅓ cup caster sugar
60ml/4 tbsp strong black coffee
30ml/2 tbsp dark rum
6 egg whites
icing sugar, for dusting

1 Preheat the oven with a baking sheet inside to 190°C/375°F/ Gas 5. Grease six 250ml/8fl oz/ 1 cup soufflé dishes with the melted butter.

2 Mix 15ml/1 tbsp of the cocoa with 15ml/1 tbsp of the caster sugar in a bowl. Tip the mixture into each of the dishes in turn, rotating them so that they are evenly coated.

3 Mix the remaining cocoa with the coffee and rum.

4 Whisk the egg whites in a clean, grease-free bowl until they form firm peaks. Whisk in the remaining caster sugar. Stir a generous spoonful of the whites into the cocoa mixture to lighten it, then gently fold in the remaining whites.

5 Spoon the mixture into the prepared dishes, smoothing the tops. Place on the hot baking sheet, and bake for 12–15 minutes or until well risen. Serve the soufflés immediately, lightly dusted with icing sugar.

COOK'S TIP

When serving the soufflés at the end of a dinner party, prepare them just before the meal is served. Pop in the oven as soon as the main course is finished and serve freshly baked.

Gingerbread Upside-down Pudding

A proper pudding goes down well on a cold winter's day. This one is quite quick and easy to make and looks very impressive.

INGREDIENTS

Serves 4–6

sunflower oil, for brushing

15ml/1 tbsp soft brown sugar

4 medium peaches, halved and stoned, or canned peach halves

8 walnut halves

For the base

130g/4½ oz/generous 1 cup wholemeal flour

2.5ml/½ tsp bicarbonate of soda

7.5ml/1½ tsp ground ginger

5ml/1 tsp ground cinnamon

115g/4oz/½ cup molasses sugar

1 egg

120ml/4fl oz/½ cup skimmed milk

50ml/2fl oz/¼ cup sunflower oil

1 Preheat the oven to 180°C/ 350°F/Gas 4. For the topping, brush the base and sides of a 23cm/9in round springform cake tin with oil. Sprinkle the sugar over the base.

2 Arrange the peaches cut-side down in the tin with a walnut half in each.

3 Sift together the flour, bicarbonate of soda, ginger and cinnamon, then stir in the sugar. Beat together the egg, milk and oil, then mix into the dry ingredients.

4 Pour the mixture evenly over the peaches and bake for 35–40 minutes, until firm to the touch. Turn out and serve hot.

Peach Cobbler

*A satisfying pudding which
combines fresh peaches with
almond-flavoured pastry.*

INGREDIENTS

Serves 6

about 1.5kg/3lb peaches, peeled and sliced

45ml/3 tbsp caster sugar

30ml/2 tbsp peach brandy

15ml/1 tbsp fresh lemon juice

15ml/1 tbsp cornflour

For the topping

115g/4oz/1 cup plain flour

7.5ml/1½ tsp baking powder

1.5ml/¼ tsp salt

40g/1½oz/¼ cup finely ground almonds

50g/2oz/¼ cup caster sugar

50g/2oz/4 tbsp butter or margarine

85ml/3fl oz/⅜ cup milk

1.5ml/¼ tsp almond essence

1 Preheat the oven to
220°C/425°F/Gas 7. In a bowl,
toss the peaches with the sugar,
peach brandy, lemon juice and
cornflour, then spoon the peach
mixture into a 2 litre/3½ pint/8 cup
baking dish.

2 For the topping, sift the flour,
baking powder and salt into a
mixing bowl. Stir in the ground
almonds and all but 1 tablespoon
of the sugar. With two knives, or a
pastry blender, cut in the butter or
margarine until the mixture
resembles coarse breadcrumbs.

3 Add the milk and almond
essence and stir until the
topping mixture is just combined.

4 Drop the topping in spoonfuls
on to the peaches. Sprinkle
the top with the remaining
tablespoon of sugar.

5 Bake until the cobbler topping
is browned, 30–35 minutes.
Serve hot with ice cream or crème
fraîche, if preferred.

Baked Apples with Caramel Sauce

The creamy caramel sauce turns this simple country dessert into a more sophisticated delicacy.

INGREDIENTS

Serves 6

3 Granny Smith apples, cored but not peeled

3 Red Delicious apples, cored but not peeled

150g/5oz/¾ cup light brown sugar

2.5ml/½ tsp grated nutmeg

1.5ml/¼ tsp freshly ground black pepper

40g/1½oz/¼ cup walnut pieces

40g/1½oz/scant ¼ cup sultanas

50g/2oz/4 tbsp butter or margarine, diced

For the caramel sauce

15g/½oz/1 tbsp butter or margarine

120ml/4fl oz/½ cup whipping cream

1 Preheat the oven to 190°C/ 375°F/Gas 5. Grease a baking tin just large enough to hold the apples.

2 With a small knife, cut at an angle to enlarge the core opening at the stem-end of each apple to about 2.5cm/1in in diameter. (The opening should resemble a funnel in shape.)

3 Arrange the apples in the prepared tin, stem-end up.

4 In a small saucepan, combine 175ml/6fl oz/¾ cup of water with the brown sugar, nutmeg and pepper. Bring the mixture to the boil, stirring. Boil for 6 minutes.

5 Mix together the walnuts and sultanas. Spoon some of the walnut-sultana mixture into the opening in each apple.

6 Top each apple with some of the diced butter or margarine.

7 Spoon the brown sugar sauce over and around the apples. Bake, basting occasionally with the sauce, until the apples are just tender, 45–50 minutes. Transfer the apples to a serving dish, reserving the brown sugar sauce in the baking tin. Keep the apples warm.

8 For the caramel sauce, mix the butter or margarine, cream and reserved brown sugar sauce in a saucepan. Bring to the boil, stirring occasionally, and simmer until thickened, about 2 minutes. Leave the sauce to cool slightly before serving.

VARIATION

Use a mixture of firm red and gold pears instead of the apples, preparing them in the same way. Cook for 10 minutes longer.

Baked Apples with Apricot Filling

An alternative stuffing mixture for baked apples, with a refreshing fruit flavour.

INGREDIENTS

Serves 6

75g/3oz/scant ½ cup chopped, ready-to-eat dried apricots
50g/2oz/½ cup chopped walnuts
5ml/1 tsp grated lemon rind
2.5ml/½ tsp ground cinnamon
90g/3½oz/½ cup soft light brown sugar
25g/1oz/2 tbsp butter, at room temperature
6 large eating apples
15ml/1 tbsp melted butter

1 Preheat the oven to 190°C/375°F/Gas 5. Place the apricots, walnuts, lemon rind and cinnamon in a bowl. Add the sugar and butter and stir until thoroughly mixed.

2 Core the apples, without cutting all the way through to the base. Peel the top of each apple and then slightly widen the top of each opening to make room for the filling.

3 Spoon the filling into the apples, packing it down lightly.

4 Place the stuffed apples in an ovenproof dish large enough to hold them all comfortably side by side.

5 Brush the apples with the melted butter. Bake for 45–50 minutes, until they are tender. Serve hot.

COOK'S TIP

Accompany with real custard, Crème Anglaise, made using cream, egg yolks, caster sugar and a few drops of vanilla essence.

Pears in Chocolate Fudge Blankets

Warm poached pears coated in a rich chocolate fudge sauce – who could resist?

INGREDIENTS

Serves 6

6 ripe eating pears
30ml/2 tbsp lemon juice
75g/3oz/scant ½ cup caster sugar
1 cinnamon stick

For the sauce
200ml/7fl oz/⅞ cup double cream
150g/5oz/scant 1 cup light muscovado
    sugar
25g/1oz/2 tbsp unsalted butter
60ml/4 tbsp golden syrup
120ml/4fl oz/½ cup milk
200g/7oz plain dark chocolate, broken
    into squares

1 Peel the pears thinly, leaving the stalks on. Scoop out the cores from the base. Brush the cut surfaces with lemon juice to prevent browning.

2 Place the sugar and 300ml/ ½ pint/1¼ cups of water in a large saucepan. Heat gently until the sugar dissolves. Add the pears and cinnamon stick with any remaining lemon juice, and, if necessary, a little more water, so that the pears are almost covered.

3 Bring to the boil, then lower the heat, cover the pan and simmer the pears gently for 15-20 minutes.

4 Meanwhile, make the sauce. Place the cream, sugar, butter, golden syrup and milk in a heavy-based saucepan. Heat gently until the sugar has dissolved and the butter and syrup have melted, then bring to the boil. Boil, stirring constantly, for about 5 minutes or until thick and smooth.

5 Remove the pan from the heat and stir in the chocolate, a few squares at a time, stirring until it has all melted.

6 Using a slotted spoon, transfer the poached pears to a dish. Keep hot. Boil the syrup rapidly to reduce to about 45–60ml/3–4 tbsp. Remove the cinnamon stick and gently stir the syrup into the chocolate sauce.

7 Serve the pears in individual bowls or on dessert plates, with the hot chocolate fudge sauce spooned over.

Sticky Toffee Pudding

Filling, warming and packed with calories, but still everyone's favourite pudding.

INGREDIENTS

Serves 6

115g/4oz/1 cup toasted walnuts, chopped
175g/6oz/¾ cup butter
175g/6oz/scant 1 cup soft brown sugar
60ml/4 tbsp single cream
30ml/2 tbsp lemon juice
2 eggs, beaten
115g/4oz/1 cup self-raising flour

1 Grease a 900ml/1½ pint/ 3¾ cup pudding basin and add half the walnuts.

2 Heat 50g/2oz/4 tbsp of the butter with 50g/2oz/4 tbsp of the sugar, the cream and 15ml/ 1 tbsp lemon juice in a small pan, stirring until smooth. Pour half into the pudding basin, then swirl to coat it a little way up the sides.

3 Beat the remaining butter and sugar until light and fluffy, then gradually beat in the eggs. Fold in the flour and the remaining nuts and lemon juice and spoon into the bowl.

4 Cover the bowl with grease-proof paper with a pleat folded in the centre, then tie securely with string.

5 Steam the pudding for about 1¼ hours, until it is set in the centre.

6 Just before serving, gently warm the remaining sauce. Unmould the pudding on to a warm plate and pour over the warm sauce.

Chocolate and Orange Soufflé

The base in this soufflé is an easy-to-make semolina mixture, rather than the thick white sauce that most soufflés call for.

INGREDIENTS

Serves 4

600ml/1 pint/2½ cups milk
50g/2oz/generous ⅓ cup semolina
50g/2oz/scant ¼ cup brown sugar
grated rind of 1 orange
90ml/6 tbsp fresh orange juice
3 eggs, separated
65g/2½oz plain chocolate, grated
icing sugar, for sprinkling

1 Preheat the oven to 200°C/400°F/Gas 6. Butter a shallow 1.75 litre/3 pint/7½ cup ovenproof dish.

2 Pour the milk into a heavy-based saucepan, sprinkle over the semolina and brown sugar, then heat, stirring the mixture all the time, until boiling and thickened.

3 Remove the pan from the heat, beat in the orange rind and juice, egg yolks and all but 15ml/ 1 tbsp of the grated chocolate.

4 Whisk the egg whites until stiff, then lightly fold into the semolina mixture in three batches. Spoon into the buttered dish and bake for about 30 minutes, until just set in the centre. Sprinkle with the reserved chocolate and the icing sugar.

Queen of Puddings

This hot pudding was developed from a seventeenth-century recipe by Queen Victoria's chefs and named in her honour.

INGREDIENTS

Serves 4

75g/3oz/1½ cups fresh breadcrumbs

60ml/4 tbsp caster sugar, plus 5ml/1 tsp

grated rind of 1 lemon

600ml/1 pint/2½ cups milk

4 eggs

45ml/3 tbsp raspberry jam, warmed

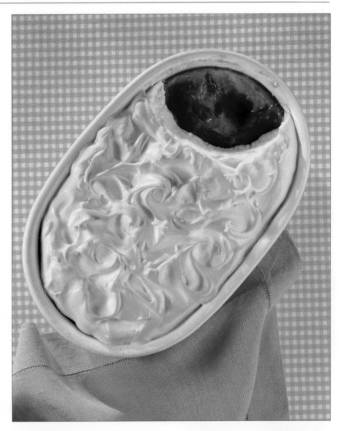

1 Preheat the oven to 160°C/325°F/Gas 3. Stir the breadcrumbs, 30ml/2 tbsp of the sugar and the lemon rind together in a bowl. Bring the milk to the boil in a saucepan, then stir into the breadcrumb mixture.

2 Separate three of the eggs and beat the yolks with the whole egg. Stir into the breadcrumb mixture, pour into a buttered baking dish and leave to stand for 30 minutes, then bake the pudding for 50–60 minutes, until set.

COOK'S TIP

Ring the changes by using another flavoured jam, lemon curd, marmalade or fruit purée.

3 Whisk the three egg whites in a large, clean bowl until stiff but not dry, then gradually whisk in the remaining 30ml/2 tbsp caster sugar until the mixture is thick and glossy, taking care not to overwhip.

4 Spread the jam over the pudding, then spoon over the meringue to cover the top completely. Sprinkle the remaining sugar over the meringue, then bake for a further 15 minutes, until the meringue is beginning to turn a light golden colour.

Apple Couscous Pudding

This unusual couscous mixture makes a delicious family pudding with a rich fruity flavour, but virtually no fat.

INGREDIENTS

Serves 4

600ml/1 pint/2½ cups apple juice
115g/4oz/⅔ cup couscous
40g/1½oz/scant ¼ cup sultanas
2.5ml/½ tsp mixed spice
1 large Bramley cooking apple, peeled,
    cored and sliced
25g/1oz/2 tbsp demerara sugar
natural low fat yogurt, to serve

1 Preheat the oven to 200°C/400°F/Gas 6. Place the apple juice, couscous, sultanas and spice in a pan and bring to the boil, stirring. Cover and simmer for 10–12 minutes, until all the free liquid is absorbed.

COOK'S TIP

To ring the changes, substitute other dried fruits for the sultanas in this recipe – try chopped dates or ready-to-eat pears, figs or apricots.

2 Spoon half the couscous mixture into a 1.2 litre/2 pint/ 5 cup ovenproof dish and top with half the apple slices. Top with the remaining couscous.

3 Arrange the remaining apple slices overlapping over the top and sprinkle with demerara sugar. Bake for 25–30 minutes, or until the apples are golden brown. Serve hot with yogurt.

Cabinet Pudding

A rich, baked custard, flavoured with glacé and dried fruit.

Serves 4

25g/1oz/2½ tbsp raisins, chopped
30ml/2 tbsp brandy (optional)
25g/1oz/2½ tbsp glacé cherries, halved
25g/1oz/2½ tbsp angelica, chopped
2 trifle sponge cakes, diced
50g/2oz ratafias, crushed
2 eggs
2 egg yolks
30ml/2 tbsp sugar
450ml/¾ pint/1⅞ cups single cream or
   milk
few drops of vanilla essence

1 Soak the raisins in the brandy, if using, for several hours.

2 Butter a 750ml/1¼ pint/3 cup charlotte mould and arrange some of the cherries and angelica in the base.

3 Mix the remaining cherries and angelica with the sponge cakes, ratafias and raisins and brandy, if using, and spoon into the mould.

4 Lightly whisk together the eggs, egg yolks and sugar. Bring the cream or milk just to the boil, then stir into the egg mixture with the vanilla essence.

5 Strain the egg mixture into the mould, then leave for 15–30 minutes.

6 Preheat the oven to 160°C/ 325°F/Gas 3. Place the mould in a roasting tin, cover with baking paper and pour in boiling water to come halfway up the side of the mould. Bake for 1 hour, or until set. Leave for 2–3 minutes, then turn out on to a warm plate, to serve.

Eve's Pudding

The tempting apples beneath the sponge topping are the reason for the pudding's name.

Serves 4–6

115g/4oz/½ cup butter
115g/4oz/generous ½ cup caster sugar
2 eggs, beaten
grated rind and juice of 1 lemon
90g/3½oz/scant 1 cup self-raising flour
40g/1½oz/⅓ cup ground almonds
115g/4oz/scant ½ cup soft brown sugar
675g/1½lb cooking apples, cored and
   thinly sliced
25g/1oz/¼ cup flaked almonds

1 Beat together the butter and caster sugar in a large mixing bowl until the mixture is very light and fluffy.

2 Gradually beat the eggs into the butter mixture, beating well after each addition, then fold in the lemon rind, flour and ground almonds.

3 Mix the brown sugar, apples and lemon juice, tip into the dish, add the sponge mixture, then the almonds. Bake for 40–45 minutes, until golden.

Chocolate Crêpes with Plums and Port

A good dinner party dessert, this dish can be made in advance and always looks impressive.

INGREDIENTS

Serves 6

50g/2oz plain chocolate, broken into
    squares
200ml/7fl oz/⅞ cup milk
120ml/4fl oz/½ cup single cream
30ml/2 tbsp cocoa powder
115g/4oz/1 cup plain flour
2 eggs

For the filling
500g/1¼lb red or golden plums
50g/2oz/¼ cup caster sugar
30ml/2 tbsp port
oil, for frying
175g/6oz/¾ cup crème fraîche

For the sauce
150g/5oz plain chocolate, broken into
    squares
175ml/6fl oz/¾ cup double cream
30ml/2 tbsp port

1 Place the chocolate in a saucepan with the milk. Heat gently until the chocolate has dissolved. Pour into a blender or food processor and add the cream, cocoa powder, flour and eggs. Process until smooth, then tip into a jug and chill for 30 minutes.

2 Meanwhile, make the filling. Halve and stone the plums. Place them in a saucepan and add the sugar and 30ml/2 tbsp of water. Bring to the boil, then lower the heat, cover, and simmer for about 10 minutes or until the plums are tender. Stir in the port; simmer for a further 30 seconds. Remove the pan from the heat and keep warm.

3 Have ready a sheet of non-stick baking paper. Heat a crêpe pan, grease it lightly with a little oil, then pour in just enough batter to cover the base of the pan, swirling to coat it evenly.

4 Cook until the crêpe has set, then flip it over to cook the other side. Slide the crêpe out on to the sheet of paper, then cook 9–11 more crêpes in the same way.

5 Make the sauce. Combine the chocolate and cream in a saucepan. Heat gently, stirring until smooth. Add the port and heat gently, stirring, for 1 minute.

6 Divide the plum filling between the crêpes, add a dollop of crème fraîche to each and roll them up carefully. Serve in shallow plates, with the chocolate sauce spooned over the top.

Chocolate Soufflé Crêpes

*A non-stick pan is ideal as it does
not need greasing between each
crêpe. Serve two crêpes per person.*

Makes 12 crêpes

75g/3oz/⅔ cup plain flour
10g/¼oz/1 tbsp unsweetened cocoa
5ml/1 tsp caster sugar
pinch of salt
5ml/1 tsp ground cinnamon
2 eggs
175ml/6fl oz/¾ cup milk
5ml/1 tsp vanilla essence
50g/2oz/4 tbsp unsalted butter, melted
icing sugar, for dusting
raspberries, pineapple and mint sprigs,
    to decorate

For the pineapple syrup

½ medium pineapple, peeled, cored and
    finely chopped
30ml/2 tbsp natural maple syrup
5ml/1 tsp cornflour
½ cinnamon stick
30ml/2 tbsp rum

For the soufflé filling

250g/9oz semi-sweet or bittersweet
    chocolate
85ml/3fl oz/⅓ cup double cream
3 eggs, separated
25g/1oz/2 tbsp caster sugar

1 Prepare the syrup. In a
saucepan over medium heat,
bring the pineapple, 125ml/4fl oz/
½ cup of water, maple syrup,
cornflour and cinnamon stick to
the boil. Simmer for 2–3 minutes
until the sauce thickens, whisking
frequently. Remove from the heat;
discard the cinnamon. Pour into
a bowl, stir in the rum and chill.

2 Prepare the crêpes. In a bowl,
sift the flour, cocoa, sugar, salt
and cinnamon. Stir to blend, then
make a well in the centre. In a
bowl, beat the eggs, milk and
vanilla. Gradually add to the well,
whisking in flour from the side to
form a smooth batter. Stir in half
the butter and pour the batter into
a jug. Allow to stand for 1 hour.

3 Heat an 18–20cm/7–8in crêpe
pan. Brush with butter. Stir the
batter. Pour 45ml/3 tbsp batter
into the pan; swirl the pan quickly
to cover the bottom with a thin
layer. Cook over medium-high
heat for 1–2 minutes until the
bottom is golden. Turn over and
cook for 30–45 seconds, then turn
on to a plate. Stack the crêpes
between non-stick baking paper.

4 Prepare the filling. In a small
saucepan, over medium heat,
melt the chocolate and cream until
smooth, stirring frequently.

5 In a bowl, beat the yolks with
half the sugar for 3–5 minutes,
until light and creamy. Gradually
beat in the chocolate mixture.
Allow to cool. In a large bowl, beat
the egg whites until soft peaks form.
Gradually beat in the remaining
sugar until stiff. Beat in a spoonful
of egg whites to the chocolate
mixture, then fold in remainder.

6 Preheat the oven to 200°C/
400°F/Gas 6. Lay a crêpe on a
plate. Spoon a little soufflé mixture
on to the crêpe, spreading it to the
edge. Fold the bottom half over the
soufflé mixture, then fold in half
again to form a filled "triangle".
Place on a buttered baking sheet.
Repeat with the remaining crêpes.

7 Brush the tops with melted
butter and bake for 15–20
minutes until fluffy. Dust with
icing sugar and garnish with raspberries, pineapple, mint and a
spoonful of pineapple syrup.

Warm Lemon and Syrup Cake

The combination of pears, sticky syrup and lemon makes this a real winner. Drizzle with single cream for extra luxury.

INGREDIENTS

Serves 8

3 eggs

175g/6oz/¾ cup butter, softened

175g/6oz/¾ cup caster sugar

175g/6oz/1½ cups self-raising flour

50g/2oz/½ cup ground almonds

1.5ml/¼ tsp freshly grated nutmeg

50g/2oz/5 tbsp candied lemon peel, finely chopped

grated rind of 1 lemon

30ml/2 tbsp lemon juice

poached pears, to serve

For the syrup

175g/6oz/¾ cup caster sugar

juice of 3 lemons

1 Preheat the oven to 180°C/350°F/Gas 4. Grease and base-line a deep, round 20cm/8in cake tin.

2 Place all the cake ingredients in a large bowl and beat well for 2–3 minutes, until the mixture is light and fluffy.

3 Tip the mixture into the prepared tin, spread level and bake for 1 hour, or until golden and firm to the touch.

4 Meanwhile, make the syrup. Put the sugar, lemon juice and 75ml/5 tbsp water in a pan. Heat gently, stirring until the sugar has dissolved, then boil, without stirring, for 1–2 minutes.

5 Turn out the cake on to a plate with a rim. Prick the surface of the cake all over with a fork, then pour over the hot syrup. Leave to soak for about 30 minutes. Serve the cake warm with thin wedges of poached pears.

Magic Chocolate Mud Pudding

A popular favourite, which magically separates into a light and luscious sponge and a velvety chocolate sauce.

INGREDIENTS

Serves 4

50g/2oz/4 tbsp butter

200g/7oz/generous 1 cup light muscovado
   sugar

475ml/16fl oz/2 cups milk

90g/3½oz/scant 1 cup self-raising flour

5ml/1 tsp ground cinnamon

75ml/5 tbsp cocoa powder

Greek-style yogurt or vanilla ice cream,
   to serve

1 Preheat the oven to 180°C/350°F/Gas 4. Lightly grease a 1.5 litre/2½ pint/6 cup ovenproof dish and place on a baking sheet.

2 Place the butter in a saucepan. Add 115g/4oz/¾ cup of the sugar and 150ml/¼ pint/⅔ cup of the milk. Heat gently, stirring from time to time, until the butter has melted and all the sugar has dissolved. Remove the pan from the heat.

COOK'S TIP
~
A soufflé dish will support the sponge as it rises above the sauce.

3 Sift the flour, cinnamon and 15ml/1 tbsp of the cocoa powder into the pan and stir into the mixture, mixing evenly. Pour the mixture into the prepared dish and level the surface.

4 Sift the remaining sugar and cocoa powder into a bowl, mix well, then sprinkle over the pudding mixture.

5 Pour the remaining milk over the pudding.

6 Bake for 45–50 minutes or until the sponge has risen to the top and is firm to the touch. Serve hot, with the yogurt or vanilla ice cream.

Christmas Pudding

This recipe makes enough to fill one 1.2 litre/2 pint/5 cup basin or two 600ml/1 pint/2½ cup basins. It can be made up to a month before Christmas and stored in a cool, dry place. Steam the pudding for 2 hours before serving. Serve with brandy or rum butter, whisky sauce, custard or whipped cream, topped with a decorative sprig of holly.

INGREDIENTS

Serves 8

115g/4oz/½ cup butter
225g/8oz/1 heaped cup soft dark brown sugar
50g/2oz/½ cup self-raising flour
5ml/1tsp ground mixed spice
1.5ml/¼ tsp grated nutmeg
2.5ml/½ tsp ground cinnamon
2 eggs
115g/4oz/2 cups fresh white breadcrumbs
175g/6oz/generous 1 cup sultanas
175g/6oz/generous 1 cup raisins
115g/4oz/½ cup currants
25g/1oz/3 tbsp mixed candied peel, chopped finely
25g/1oz/¼ cup chopped almonds
1 small cooking apple, peeled, cored and coarsely grated
finely grated rind or 1 orange or lemon
juice of 1 orange or lemon, made up to 150ml/¼ pint/⅔ cup with brandy, rum or sherry

1 Cut a disc of greaseproof paper to fit the base of the basin(s) and butter the disc and basin(s).

2 Whisk the butter and sugar together until soft. Beat in the flour, spices and eggs. Stir in the remaining ingredients thoroughly. The mixture should have a soft dropping consistency.

3 Turn the mixture into the greased basin(s) and level the top with a spoon.

4 Cover with another disc of buttered greaseproof paper.

5 Make a pleat across the centre of a large piece of greaseproof paper and cover the basin(s) with it, tying it in place with string under the rim. Cut off the excess paper. Pleat a piece of foil in the same way and cover the basin(s) with it, tucking it around the bowl neatly, under the greaseproof frill. Tie another piece of string around and across the top, as a handle.

6 Place the basin(s) in a steamer over a pan of simmering water and steam for 6 hours. Alternatively, put the basin(s) into a large pan and pour round enough boiling water to come halfway up the basin(s) and cover the pan with a tight-fitting lid. Check the water is simmering and top it up with boiling water as it evaporates. When the pudding(s) have cooked, leave to cool completely. Then remove the foil and greaseproof paper. Wipe the basin(s) clean and replace the greaseproof paper and foil with clean pieces, ready for reheating.

TO SERVE

Steam for 2 hours. Turn on to a plate and leave to stand for 5 minutes, before removing the pudding basin (the steam will rise to the top of the basin and help to loosen the pudding). Decorate with a sprig of holly.

Steamed Chocolate and Fruit Puddings

Some things always turn out well, including these wonderful little puddings. Dark, fluffy chocolate sponge with tangy cranberries and apple is served with a honeyed chocolate syrup.

INGREDIENTS

Serves 4

115g/4oz/⅔ cup dark muscovado sugar

1 eating apple

75g/3oz/¾ cup cranberries, thawed if frozen

115g/4oz/½ cup soft margarine

2 eggs

75g/3oz/⅔ cup plain flour

2.5ml/½ tsp baking powder

45ml/3 tbsp cocoa powder

For the chocolate syrup

115g/4oz plain chocolate, broken into squares

30ml/2 tbsp clear honey

15ml/1 tbsp unsalted butter

2.5ml/½ tsp vanilla essence

1 Prepare a steamer or half fill a saucepan with water and bring it to the boil. Grease four individual pudding basins and sprinkle each one with a little of the muscovado sugar to coat well all over.

2 Peel and core the apple. Dice it into a bowl, add the cranberries and mix well. Divide equally among the prepared pudding basins.

3 Place the remaining muscovado sugar in a mixing bowl. Add the margarine, eggs, flour, baking powder and cocoa; beat until combined and smooth.

4 Spoon the mixture into the basins and cover each with a double thickness of foil. Steam for about 45 minutes, topping up the boiling water as required, until the puddings are well risen and firm.

5 Make the syrup. Mix the chocolate, honey, butter and vanilla essence in a small saucepan. Heat gently, stirring, until melted and smooth.

6 Run a knife around the edge of each pudding to loosen it, then turn out on to individual plates. Serve at once, with the chocolate syrup.

COOK'S TIP

The puddings can be cooked very quickly in the microwave. Use non-metallic basins and cover with greaseproof paper instead of foil. Cook on High (100% power) for 5–6 minutes, then stand for 2–3 minutes before turning out.

Hot Chocolate Cake

This is wonderfully wicked served as a pudding with a white chocolate sauce. The basic cake freezes well – thaw, then warm in the microwave before serving.

Makes 10–12 slices

200g/7oz/1¾ cups self-raising wholemeal flour
25g/1oz/¼ cup cocoa powder
pinch of salt
175g/6oz/¾ cup soft margarine
175g/6oz/¾ cup soft light brown sugar
few drops vanilla essence
4 eggs
75g/3oz white chocolate, roughly chopped
chocolate leaves and curls, to decorate

For the white chocolate sauce
75g/3oz white chocolate
150ml/¼ pint/⅔ cup single cream
30–45ml/2–3 tbsp milk

1 Preheat the oven to 160°C/ 325°F/Gas 3. Sift the flour, cocoa powder and salt into a bowl, adding in the whole wheat flakes from the sieve.

2 Cream the margarine, sugar and vanilla essence together until light and fluffy, then gently beat in one egg.

3 Gradually stir in the remaining eggs, one at a time, alternately folding in some of the flour, until the mixture is blended in.

4 Stir in the white chocolate and spoon into a greased 675–900g/1½–2lb loaf tin or an 18cm/7in greased cake tin. Bake for 30–40 minutes, or until just firm to the touch and shrinking away from the sides of the tin.

5 Meanwhile, prepare the sauce. Heat the white chocolate and cream very gently in a pan until the chocolate is melted. Add the milk and stir until cool.

6 Serve the cake sliced, in a pool of sauce and decorated with chocolate leaves and curls.

Chocolate Almond Meringue Pie

This dream dessert combines three very popular flavours: velvety chocolate filling on a light orange pastry case, topped with fluffy meringue.

Serves 6

175g/6oz/1½ cups plain flour
50g/2oz/⅓ cup ground rice
150g/5oz/⅔ cup unsalted butter
finely grated rind of 1 orange
1 egg yolk
flaked almonds and melted plain dark
   chocolate, to decorate

For the filling
150g/5oz plain dark chocolate, broken
   into squares
50g/2oz/4 tbsp unsalted butter, softened
75g/3oz/⅓ cup caster sugar
10ml/2 tsp cornflour
4 egg yolks
75g/3oz/¾ cup ground almonds

For the meringue
3 egg whites
150g/5oz/¾ cup caster sugar

1 Sift the flour and ground rice into a bowl. Rub in the butter until the mixture resembles breadcrumbs. Stir in the orange rind. Add the egg yolk; bring the dough together. Roll out and use to line a 23cm/9in round flan tin. Chill for 30 minutes.

2 Preheat the oven to 190°C/375°F/Gas 5. Prick the pastry base all over with a fork, cover with greaseproof paper weighed down with baking beans and bake blind for 10 minutes. Remove the pastry case; take out the baking beans and paper.

3 Make the filling. Melt the chocolate in a heatproof bowl over hot water. Cream the butter with the sugar in a bowl, then beat in the cornflour and egg yolks. Fold in the almonds, then the chocolate. Spread in the pastry case. Bake for a further 10 minutes.

4 Make the meringue. Whisk the egg whites until stiff, then gradually add half the caster sugar. Fold in remaining sugar.

5 Spoon the meringue over the chocolate filling, lifting if up with the back of the spoon to form peaks. Reduce the oven temperature to 180°C/350°F/Gas 4 and bake the pie for 15–20 minutes or until the topping is pale gold. Serve warm, scattered with almonds and drizzled with melted chocolate.

Chocolate Chip and Banana Pudding

Hot and steamy, this superb light pudding tastes extra special served with chocolate sauce.

INGREDIENTS

Serves 4

200g/7oz/1¾ cups self-raising flour

75g/3oz/6 tbsp unsalted butter or
   margarine

2 ripe bananas

75g/3oz/⅓ cup caster sugar

60ml/4 tbsp milk

1 egg, beaten

60ml/4 tbsp plain chocolate chips or
   chopped chocolate

Glossy Chocolate Sauce and whipped
   cream, to serve

1 Prepare a steamer or half fill a saucepan with water and bring it to the boil. Grease a 1 litre/1¾ pint/4 cup pudding basin. Sift the flour into a bowl and rub in the butter or margarine until the mixture resembles breadcrumbs.

2 Mash the bananas in a bowl. Stir them into the creamed mixture, with the caster sugar.

3 Whisk the milk with the egg in a jug or bowl, then beat into the pudding mixture. Stir in the chocolate chips or chopped chocolate.

4 Spoon the mixture into the prepared basin, cover closely with a double thickness of foil, and steam for 2 hours, topping up the water as required during cooking.

5 Run a knife around the top of the pudding to loosen it, then turn it out on to a warm serving dish. Serve hot, with the chocolate sauce and a spoonful of whipped cream.

COOK'S TIP

If you have a food processor, make a quick-mix version by processing all the ingredients, except the chocolate, until smooth. Stir in the chocolate and proceed as in the recipe.

Hot Plum Batter Pudding

Other fruits can be used in place of plums, depending on the season. Canned black cherries are a convenient substitute to keep in the store cupboard.

INGREDIENTS

Serves 4

450g/1lb ripe red plums, quartered and stoned
200ml/7fl oz/⅞ cup skimmed milk
60ml/4 tbsp skimmed milk powder
15ml/1 tbsp light muscovado sugar
5ml/1 tsp vanilla essence
75g/3oz/⅔ cup self-raising flour
2 egg whites
icing sugar, to sprinkle

1 Preheat the oven to 220°C/ 425°F/Gas 7. Lightly oil a wide, shallow ovenproof dish and add the plums.

2 Pour the milk, milk powder, sugar, vanilla, flour and egg whites into a blender or food processor. Process until smooth.

3 Pour the batter over the plums. Bake for 25–30 minutes, or until puffed and golden. Sprinkle with icing sugar and serve immediately.

COOK'S TIP

If you don't have a food processor, then place the dry ingredients for the batter in a large bowl and gradually whisk in the milk and egg whites.

Glazed Apricot Sponge

Proper puddings can be very high in saturated fat, but this healthy version uses the minimum of oil and no eggs.

INGREDIENTS

Serves 4

10ml/2 tsp golden syrup
411g/14½oz can apricot halves in fruit juice
150g/5oz/1¼ cups self-raising flour
75g/3oz/1½ cups fresh breadcrumbs
90g/3½oz/½ cup light muscovado sugar
5ml/1 tsp ground cinnamon
30ml/2 tbsp sunflower oil
175ml/6fl oz/¾ cup skimmed milk

1 Preheat the oven to 180°C/ 350°F/Gas 4. Lightly oil a 900ml/1½ pint/3¾ cup pudding basin. Spoon in the syrup.

2 Drain the apricots and reserve the juice. Arrange about 8 halves in the basin. Purée the rest of the apricots with the juice and set aside.

3 Mix the flour, breadcrumbs, sugar and cinnamon then beat in the oil and milk. Spoon into the basin and bake for 50–55 minutes, or until firm and golden. Turn out and serve with the puréed fruit as an accompaniment.

QUICK AND EASY

Frudités with Honey Dip

A colourful and tasty variation on the popular savoury crudités.

INGREDIENTS

Serves 4

225g/8oz/1 cup Greek-style yogurt

45ml/3 tbsp clear honey

selection of fresh fruit for dipping such as
    apples, pears, tangerines, grapes, figs,
    cherries, strawberries and kiwi fruit

1 Place the yogurt in a dish, beat until smooth, then partially stir in the honey, leaving a little marbled effect.

2 Cut the various fruits into wedges or bite-sized pieces or leave whole.

3 Arrange the fruits on a platter with the bowl of dip in the centre. Serve chilled.

COOK'S TIP

Sprinkle the apple and pear
wedges with lemon juice to
prevent discolouring.

Watermelon, Ginger and Grapefruit Salad

*This pretty, pink combination is
very light and refreshing for any
summer meal.*

INGREDIENTS

Serves 4

500g/1lb/2 cups diced watermelon flesh

2 ruby or pink grapefruit

2 pieces stem ginger in syrup

30ml/2 tbsp stem ginger syrup

whipped cream, to serve

1 Remove any seeds from the
watermelon and cut into bite-
sized chunks.

2 Using a small sharp knife, cut
away all the peel and white
pith from the grapefruit and
carefully lift out the segments,
catching any juice in a bowl.

COOK'S TIP
〜
Toss the fruits gently – grapefruit
segments will break up easily
and the appearance of the dish
will be spoiled.

3 Finely chop the stem ginger
and place in a serving bowl
with the melon cubes and
grapefruit segments, adding the
reserved juice.

4 Spoon over the ginger syrup
and toss the fruits lightly to
mix evenly. Chill before serving
with a bowl of whipped cream.

Yogurt with Apricots and Pistachios

If you allow a thick yogurt to drain overnight, it becomes even thicker and more luscious. Add honeyed apricots and nuts and you have an exotic yet simple dessert.

Serves 4

450g/1lb Greek-style yogurt
175g/6oz/⅔ cup no-need-to-soak dried
    apricots, snipped
15ml/1 tbsp clear honey
orange rind, grated
30ml/2 tbsp unsalted pistachios, roughly
    chopped
ground cinnamon

1 Place the yogurt in a fine sieve and allow it to drain overnight in the fridge over a bowl.

2 Discard the whey from the yogurt. Place the apricots in a saucepan, barely cover with water and simmer for just 3 minutes, to soften. Drain and cool, then mix with the honey.

3 Mix the yogurt with the apricots, orange rind and nuts. Spoon into sundae dishes, sprinkle over a little cinnamon and chill.

VARIATION

For a simple dessert, strain the fruit, cover with yogurt and sprinkle with demerara sugar and a little mixed spice or cinnamon.

Fresh Pineapple Salad

Very refreshing, this salad can be prepared ahead. Orange flower water is available from Middle Eastern food stores or good delicatessens.

Serves 4

1 small ripe pineapple
icing sugar, to taste
15ml/1 tbsp orange flower water, or more
    if liked
115g/4oz/good ½ cup fresh dates, stoned
    and quartered
225g/8oz fresh strawberries, sliced
few fresh mint sprigs, to decorate

1 Cut the skin from the pineapple and, using the tip of a vegetable peeler, remove as many brown "eyes" as possible. Quarter lengthways, remove the core, then slice.

2 Lay the pineapple in a shallow glass bowl. Sprinkle with sugar and orange flower water.

3 Add the dates and strawberries to the pineapple, cover and chill for at least 2 hours, stirring once or twice. Serve lightly chilled decorated with a few mint sprigs.

Figs with Ricotta Cream

Fresh, ripe figs are full of natural sweetness, and need little adornment. This simple recipe makes the most of their beautiful, intense flavour.

INGREDIENTS

Serves 4

4 ripe, fresh figs

115g/4oz/½ cup ricotta or cottage cheese

45ml/3 tbsp crème fraîche

15ml/1 tbsp clear honey

2.5ml/½ tsp vanilla essence

freshly grated nutmeg, to decorate

3 Mix together the ricotta or cottage cheese, crème fraîche, honey and vanilla.

4 Spoon a little ricotta cream on to each plate and sprinkle with grated nutmeg to serve.

1 Trim the stalks from the figs. Make four cuts through each fig from the stalk-end, cutting them almost through but leaving them joined at the base.

2 Place the figs on serving plates and open them out.

Three-fruits Compote

Mixing dried fruits with fresh ones makes a good combination, especially if flavoured delicately with a little orange flower water. A melon-ball scoop gives the compote a classy touch, but you could chop the melon into cubes.

Serves 6

175g/6oz/¾ cup no-need-to-soak, dried
   apricots
1 small ripe pineapple
1 small ripe melon
15ml/1 tbsp orange flower water
sprig of mint, to decorate

1 Put the apricots into a saucepan with 300ml/½ pint/ 1¼ cups of water. Bring to the boil, then simmer for 5 minutes. Set aside to cool.

2 Peel and quarter the pineapple then cut the core from each quarter and discard. Cut the flesh into chunks.

3 Seed the melon and scoop balls from the flesh. Save any juices which fall from the fruits and tip them into the apricots.

4 Stir in the orange flower water and mix all the fruits together. Pour into a serving dish, decorate with mint and chill lightly.

VARIATION

A good fruit salad needn't be a boring mixture of multi-coloured fruits swimming in sweet syrup. Instead of the usual apple, orange and grape type of salad, give it a theme, such as red berry fruits or a variety of sliced green fruits – even a dish of just one fruit nicely prepared and sprinkled lightly with some sugar and fresh lemon juice can look beautiful and tastes delicious. Do not use more than three fruits in a salad so that the flavours remain distinct.

Prune and Orange Pots

A simple, storecupboard dessert, made in minutes. It can be served straight away, but it's best chilled for about half an hour before serving.

Serves 4

225g/8oz/1 cup ready-to-eat dried prunes
150ml/¼ pint/⅔ cup orange juice
225g/8oz/1 cup low-fat natural yogurt
shreds of orange rind, to decorate

1 Remove the stones from the prunes and roughly chop them. Place them in a pan with the orange juice.

2 Bring the juice to the boil, stirring. Reduce the heat, cover and leave to simmer for 5 minutes, until the prunes are tender and the liquid is reduced by half.

3 Remove from the heat, allow to cool slightly and then beat well with a wooden spoon, until the fruit breaks down to a rough purée.

4 Transfer the mixture to a bowl. Stir in the yogurt, swirling the yogurt and fruit purée together lightly, to give an attractive marbled effect.

5 Spoon the mixture into stemmed glasses or individual dishes, smoothing the tops.

6 Top each dish with a few shreds of orange rind, to decorate. Chill before serving.

VARIATION

This dessert can also be made with other ready-to-eat dried fruit, such as apricots or peaches. For a special occasion, add a dash of brandy or Cointreau with the yogurt.

Quick Apricot Blender Whip

One of the quickest desserts you could make – as well as being one of the prettiest.

Serves 4

400g/14oz can apricot halves in juice
15ml/1 tbsp Grand Marnier or brandy
175g/6oz/¾ cup Greek-style yogurt
30ml/2 tbsp flaked almonds

1 Drain the juice from the apricots and place the fruit and liqueur in a blender or food processor.

2 Process the apricots to a smooth purée.

COOK'S TIP

For an even lighter dessert, use low-fat instead of Greek yogurt, and a little fruit juice from the can instead of liqueur.

3 Spoon the fruit purée and yogurt in alternate spoonfuls into four tall glasses or glass dishes, swirling them together slightly to give a marbled effect.

4 Lightly toast the almonds until they are golden. Let them cool slightly and then sprinkle them over the top.

Emerald Fruit Salad

This mixture of green and golden fruit both looks and tastes refreshing.

INGREDIENTS

Serves 4

30ml/2 tbsp lime juice

30ml/2 tbsp clear honey

2 green eating apples, cored and sliced

1 small ripe Ogen melon, diced

2 kiwi fruit, sliced

1 star fruit, sliced

mint sprigs, to decorate

yogurt or fromage frais, to serve

1 Mix together the lime juice and honey in a large bowl, then toss the apple slices in this.

2 Carefully stir in the melon, kiwi fruit and star fruit. Place in a glass serving dish and chill before serving.

3 Decorate with mint sprigs and serve with yogurt or fromage frais, if preferred.

> ### COOK'S TIP
> ❧
> Star fruit is best when fully ripe – look for plump, yellow fruit.

Peach and Ginger Paskha

This simpler adaptation of a Russian Easter favourite is made with much lighter ingredients than the traditional version.

INGREDIENTS

Serves 4–6

350g/12oz/1½ cups low fat cottage cheese

2 ripe peaches or nectarines

90g/3½oz/scant ⅓ cup low fat natural
   yogurt

2 pieces stem ginger in syrup, drained and
   chopped

30ml/2 tbsp stem ginger syrup

2.5ml/½ tsp vanilla essence

peach slices and toasted flaked almonds,
   to decorate

1 Drain the cottage cheese and rub through a sieve into a bowl. Stone and roughly chop the peaches or nectarines.

2 Mix together the chopped peaches or nectarines, cottage cheese, yogurt, ginger, syrup and vanilla essence.

3 Line a new, clean flowerpot or a sieve with a piece of clean, fine cloth such as muslin.

4 Tip in the cheese mixture, then wrap over the cloth and place a weight on top. Leave over a bowl in a cool place to drain overnight. To serve, unwrap the cloth and invert the paskha on to a plate. Decorate with peach slices and almonds.

Raspberry and Passion Fruit Swirls

If passion fruit is not available, this simple dessert can be made with raspberries alone.

INGREDIENTS

Serves 4

300g/11oz/scant 2 cups raspberries
2 passion fruit
400g/14oz/1⅔ cups low-fat fromage frais
30ml/2 tbsp granulated sugar
raspberries and sprigs of mint, to decorate

1 Mash the raspberries in a small bowl with a fork until the juice runs. Scoop out the passion fruit pulp into a separate bowl with the fromage frais and sugar and mix together thoroughly.

COOK'S TIP

Over-ripe, slightly soft fruit can also be used in this recipe. You could use frozen raspberries when fresh are not available, but thaw them first.

2 Spoon alternate spoonfuls of the raspberry pulp and the fromage frais mixture into stemmed glasses or one large serving dish, stirring lightly to create a swirled effect.

3 Decorate each dessert with a whole raspberry and a sprig of fresh mint. Serve chilled.

VARIATION

Other summer fruits would be just as delicious – try a mix of strawberries and redcurrants with the raspberries, or use mangoes, peaches or apricots, which you will need to purée in a food processor or blender before mixing with the fromage frais.

Raspberry Muesli Layer

As well as being a delicious, low-fat, high-fibre dessert, this can also be served for a quick, healthy breakfast.

INGREDIENTS

Serves 4

225g/8oz/1⅓ cups fresh or frozen and
    thawed raspberries
225g/8oz/1 cup low-fat natural yogurt
75g/3oz/¾ cup Swiss-style muesli

3 Sprinkle a generous layer of muesli over the yogurt.

4 Repeat with the raspberries and other ingredients. Top each with a whole raspberry.

1 Reserve four raspberries for decoration, and then spoon a few raspberries into four stemmed glasses or glass dishes.

2 Top the raspberries with a spoonful of yogurt in each glass.

COOK'S TIP

This recipe can be made in advance and stored in the fridge for several hours, or overnight if you're serving it for breakfast.

Almost Instant Banana Pudding

Banana and ginger make a great combination in this very fast dessert.

INGREDIENTS

Serves 6–8

4 thick slices ginger cake
6 bananas
30ml/2 tbsp lemon juice
300ml/½ pint/1¼ cups whipping cream or
    fromage frais
60ml/4 tbsp fruit juice
30–45ml/3–4 tbsp soft brown sugar

1 Break up the cake into chunks and arrange in an ovenproof dish. Slice the bananas and toss in the lemon juice.

2 Whip the cream and, when firm, gently whip in the juice. (If using fromage frais, just gently stir in the juice.) Fold in the bananas and spoon the mixture over the ginger cake.

3 Top with the soft brown sugar and place under a hot grill for 2–3 minutes to caramelize. Chill to set firm again if you wish, or serve when required.

Ginger and Orange Crème Brûlée

This is a useful way of cheating at crème brûlée! Most people would never know unless you overchill the custard, or keep it more than a day, but there's little risk of that!

INGREDIENTS

Serves 4–5

2 eggs, plus 2 egg yolks
300ml/½ pint/1¼ cups single cream
30ml/2 tbsp caster sugar
5ml/1 tsp powdered gelatine or alternative
finely grated rind and juice of ½ orange
1 large piece stem ginger, finely chopped
45–60ml/3–4 tbsp icing or caster sugar
orange segments and sprig of mint,
    to decorate

COOK'S TIP

For a milder ginger flavour, just add up to 5ml/1 tsp ground ginger instead of the stem ginger.

1 Whisk the eggs and yolks together until pale. Bring the cream and sugar to the boil, remove from the heat and sprinkle on the gelatine. Stir until the gelatine has dissolved and then pour the cream mixture on to the eggs, whisking all the time.

2 Add the orange rind, a little juice to taste, and the chopped ginger to the mixture.

3 Pour into four or five ramekins and chill until set.

4 Some time before serving, sprinkle the sugar generously over the top of the custard and put under a very hot grill. Watch closely for the couple of moments it takes for the tops to caramelize. Allow to cool before serving. Decorate with a few segments of orange and a sprig of mint.

Pineapple Flambé

Flambéing means adding alcohol and then burning it off so the flavour is not too overpowering. This recipe is just as good, however, without the brandy – perfect if you wish to serve it to young children.

INGREDIENTS

Serves 4

1 large, ripe pineapple
40g/1½oz/3 tbsp unsalted butter
40g/1½oz/3 tbsp brown sugar
60ml/4 tbsp fresh orange juice
30ml/2 tbsp brandy or vodka
25g/1oz/4 tbsp slivered almonds, toasted

1 Cut away the top and base of the pineapple. Then cut down the sides, removing all the dark "eyes", but leaving the pineapple in a good shape.

2 Cut the pineapple into thin slices and, with an apple corer, remove the hard central core.

3 In a large frying pan melt the butter, sugar and orange juice. Add the pineapple slices and cook for about 1–2 minutes, turning once to coat both sides.

4 Add the brandy or vodka and light with a match immediately. Let the flames die down and then sprinkle with the toasted almonds.

Warm Pears in Cider

This is an excellent pudding for an autumn day.

INGREDIENTS

Serves 4

1 lemon
50g/2oz/¼ cup caster sugar
a little grated nutmeg
250ml/8fl oz/1 cup sweet cider
4 firm, ripe pears
freshly made custard, cream or ice cream,
    to serve

1 Carefully remove the rind from the lemon with a potato peeler leaving any white pith behind.

2 Squeeze the juice from the lemon into a saucepan, add the rind, sugar, nutmeg and cider and heat through to dissolve the sugar.

3 Carefully peel the pears, leaving the stalks on if possible, and place them in the pan of cider. Poach the pears for 10–15 minutes until almost tender, turning them frequently to cook evenly.

4 Transfer the pears to individual serving dishes using a slotted spoon. Simmer the liquid over a high heat until it reduces slightly and becomes syrupy.

5 Pour the warm syrup over the pears, and serve at once with freshly made custard, cream or ice cream.

COOK'S TIP

To get pears of just the right firmness, you may have to buy them slightly under-ripe and then wait a day or more. Soft pears are no good at all for this dish.

Chocolate Fudge Sundaes

They look impressive, taste fantastic and only take minutes to make.

INGREDIENTS

Serves 4

4 scoops each vanilla and coffee ice cream
2 small ripe bananas, sliced
whipped cream
toasted flaked almonds

For the sauce

50g/2oz/¼ cup soft light brown sugar
120ml/4fl/oz/½ cup golden syrup
45ml/3 tbsp strong black coffee
5ml/1 tsp ground cinnamon
150g/5oz plain chocolate, chopped
85ml/3fl oz/⅓ cup whipping cream
45ml/3 tbsp coffee liqueur (optional)

1 To make the sauce, place the sugar, syrup, coffee and cinnamon in a heavy-based saucepan. Bring to the boil, then boil for about 5 minutes, stirring the mixture constantly.

2 Turn off the heat and stir in the chocolate. When melted and smooth, stir in the cream and liqueur, if using. Leave the sauce to cool slightly. If made ahead, reheat the sauce gently until just warm.

3 Fill four glasses with one scoop of vanilla and another of coffee ice cream.

4 Scatter the sliced bananas over the ice cream. Pour the warm fudge sauce over the bananas, then top each sundae with a generous swirl of whipped cream. Sprinkle toasted almonds over the cream and serve at once.

VARIATION

Ring the changes by choosing other flavours of ice cream such as strawberry, toffee or chocolate. In the summer, substitute raspberries or strawberries for the bananas, and scatter chopped roasted hazelnuts on top in place of the flaked almonds.

Brazilian Coffee Bananas

*Rich, lavish and sinful-looking, this
dessert takes only about two minutes
to make!*

INGREDIENTS

Serves 4

4 small ripe bananas
15ml/1 tbsp instant coffee granules or
    powder
30ml/2 tbsp dark muscovado sugar
250g/9oz/1⅛ cups Greek-style yogurt
15ml/1 tbsp toasted flaked almonds

1 Peel and slice one banana and
mash the remaining three with
a fork.

2 Dissolve the coffee in 15ml/
1 tbsp of hot water and stir
into the mashed bananas.

3 Spoon a little of the mashed
banana mixture into four
serving dishes and sprinkle with
sugar. Top with a spoonful of
yogurt, then repeat until all the
ingredients are used up.

4 Swirl the last layer of yogurt
for a marbled effect. Finish
with a few banana slices and flaked
almonds. Serve cold. Best eaten
within about an hour of making.

VARIATION

For a special occasion, add a dash
of dark rum or brandy to the
bananas for extra richness.

Orange Yogurt Brûlées

A luxurious treat, but one that is much lower in fat than the classic brûlées, which are made with cream, eggs and lots of sugar.

Serves 4

2 medium oranges

150g/5oz/⅔ cup Greek-style yogurt

50g/2oz/¼ cup crème fraîche

45ml/3 tbsp golden caster sugar

30ml/2 tbsp light muscovado sugar

3 Mix together the two sugars and sprinkle them evenly over the tops of the dishes.

4 Place the dishes under a preheated, very hot grill for 3–4 minutes or until the sugar melts and turns into a rich golden brown. Serve warm or cold.

1 With a sharp knife, cut away all the peel and white pith from the oranges and chop the fruit. Or, if there's time, segment the oranges, carefully removing all the membrane.

2 Place the fruit in the bottom of four individual flameproof dishes. Mix together the yogurt and crème fraîche and spoon the mixture over the oranges.

Grilled Pineapple with Rum Custard

Freshly ground black pepper may seem an unusual ingredient to put with pineapple, until you realise that peppercorns are the fruit of a tropical vine. If the idea does not appeal, leave out the pepper.

INGREDIENTS

Serves 4

1 ripe pineapple
25g/1oz/2tbsp butter
fresh strawberries, sliced, to serve
a few pineapple leaves, to decorate

For the sauce

1 egg
2 egg yolks
30ml/2 tbsp caster sugar
30ml/2 tbsp dark rum
2.5ml/½ tsp freshly ground black pepper

1 Remove the top and bottom from the pineapple with a serrated knife. Pare away the outer skin from top to bottom, remove the core and cut into slices.

2 Preheat a moderate grill. Dot the pineapple slices with butter and grill for about 5 minutes.

3 To make the sauce, place all the ingredients in a bowl. Set over a saucepan of simmering water and whisk with a hand-held mixer for about 3–4 minutes or until foamy and cooked. Scatter the strawberries over the pineapple, decorate with a few pineapple leaves and serve with the sauce.

COOK'S TIP

The sweetest pineapples are picked and exported when ripe. Contrary to popular belief, pineapples do not ripen well after picking. Choose fruit that smells sweet and yields to firm pressure from your thumbs.

Banana and Passion Fruit Whip

This very easy and quickly prepared dessert is delicious served with crisp shortcake or ginger biscuits.

INGREDIENTS

Serves 4

2 ripe bananas

2 passion fruit

90ml/6 tbsp fromage frais

150ml/¼ pint/⅔ cup double cream

10ml/2 tsp clear honey

shortcake or ginger biscuits, to serve

1 Peel the bananas, then mash them with a fork in a bowl to a smooth purée.

2 Halve the passion fruit and scoop out the pulp. Mix with the bananas and fromage frais. Whip the cream with the honey until it forms soft peaks.

3 Carefully fold the cream and honey mixture into the fruit mixture. Spoon into four glass dishes and serve at once with shortcake or ginger biscuits.

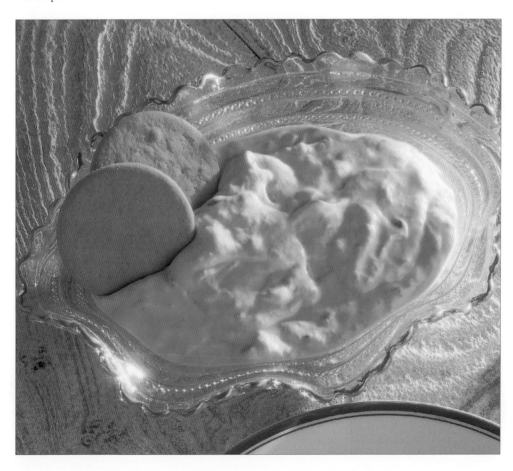

Cinnamon and Apricot Soufflés

Don't expect this to be difficult just because it's a soufflé – it really couldn't be easier, and, best of all, it's very low in calories.

INGREDIENTS

Serves 4

3 eggs

115g/4oz/½ cup apricot fruit spread

finely grated rind of ½ lemon

5ml/1 tsp ground cinnamon

extra cinnamon, to decorate

1 Preheat the oven to 190°C/375°F/Gas 5. Lightly grease four individual soufflé dishes and dust them lightly with flour.

2 Separate the eggs and place the yolks in a bowl with the fruit spread, lemon rind and cinnamon.

3 Whisk hard until the mixture is thick and pale in colour.

4 Place the egg whites in a clean bowl and whisk them until they form soft peaks.

5 Using a metal spoon or spatula, fold the egg whites evenly into the yolk mixture.

6 Divide the soufflé mixture between the prepared dishes and bake for 10–15 minutes, until well-risen and golden brown. Serve immediately, dusted with a little extra ground cinnamon.

Low
Calorie

Fresh Citrus Jelly

Fresh fruit jellies really are worth the effort – they're packed with fresh flavour, natural colour and vitamins – and they make a lovely fat-free dessert.

Serves 4

3 medium oranges

1 lemon

1 lime

75g/3oz/⅓ cup golden caster sugar

15ml/1 tbsp/1 sachet powdered gelatine, or alternative

extra slices of fruit, to decorate

1 With a sharp knife, cut all the peel and white pith from one orange and carefully remove the segments. Arrange the segments in the base of a 900ml/1½ pint/3¾ cup mould or dish.

2 Remove some shreds of citrus rind with a zester and reserve them for decoration. Grate the remaining rind from the lemon and lime and one orange. Place all the grated rind in a pan, with the sugar and 300ml/½ pint/1¼ cups of water.

3 Heat gently until the sugar has dissolved, without boiling. Remove from the heat. Squeeze the juice from all the rest of the fruit and stir it into the pan.

4 Strain the liquid into a measuring jug to remove the rind (you should have about 600ml/1 pint/2½ cups: if necessary, make up the amount with water). Sprinkle the gelatine over the liquid and stir until it has completely dissolved.

5 Pour a little of the jelly over the orange segments and chill until set. Leave the remaining jelly at room temperature to cool, but do not allow it to set.

6 Pour the remaining cooled jelly into the dish and chill until set. To serve, turn out the jelly and decorate it with the reserved citrus rind shreds and slices of citrus fruit.

Mandarins in Orange Flower Syrup

*Mandarins, tangerines, clementines,
mineolas: any of these lovely citrus
fruits are suitable for this recipe.*

INGREDIENTS

Serves 4

10 mandarins
15ml/1 tbsp icing sugar
10ml/2 tsp orange flower water
15ml/1 tbsp chopped pistachio nuts

1 Thinly pare a little of the
coloured rind from one
mandarin and cut it into fine
shreds for decoration. Squeeze the
juice from two mandarins and
reserve it.

2 Peel the remaining fruit,
removing as much of the
white pith as possible. Arrange the
whole fruits in a wide dish.

3 Mix the reserved juice, sugar
and orange flower water and
pour it over the fruit. Cover the
dish and chill for at least 1 hour.

4 Blanch the shreds of rind in
boiling water for 30 seconds.
Drain, leave to cool and sprinkle
them over the mandarins, with the
pistachio nuts, to serve.

COOK'S TIP

The mandarins look very attractive if you leave them whole,
especially if there is a large
quantity for a special occasion,
but you may prefer to separate
the segments.

Minted Raspberry Bavarois

A sophisticated dessert that can be made a day in advance for a special dinner party.

Serves 6

450g/1lb/2⅔ cups fresh or frozen and
   thawed raspberries
30ml/2 tbsp icing sugar
30ml/2 tbsp lemon juice
15ml/1 tbsp finely chopped fresh mint
30ml/2 tbsp/2 sachets powdered gelatine,
   or alternative
300ml/½ pint/1¼ cups custard, made with
   skimmed milk
250g/9oz/1⅛ cups Greek-style yogurt
fresh mint sprigs, to decorate

1 Reserve a few raspberries for
decoration. Place the
raspberries, icing sugar and lemon
juice in a blender or food processor
and process them until smooth.

2 Press the purée through a
sieve to remove the raspberry
pips. Add the mint. You should
have about 600ml/1 pint/2½ cups
of purée.

3 Sprinkle 5ml/1 tsp of the
gelatine over 30ml/2 tbsp of
boiling water and stir until the
gelatine has dissolved. Stir into
150ml/¼ pint/⅔ cup of the fruit
purée.

4 Pour this jelly into a 1 litre/
1¾ pint/4 cup mould, and
leave the mould to chill in the
fridge until the jelly is just on the
point of setting. Tip the tin to swirl
the setting jelly around the sides,
and then leave to chill until the
jelly has set completely.

5 Stir the remaining fruit purée
into the custard and yogurt.
Dissolve the rest of the gelatine in
45ml/3 tbsp of boiling water and
stir it in quickly.

6 Pour the raspberry custard
into the mould and leave it to
chill until it has set completely. To
serve, dip the mould quickly into
hot water and then turn it out and
decorate it with the reserved
raspberries and the mint sprigs.

Fruited Rice Ring

This unusual rice pudding looks
beautiful turned out of a ring mould
but if you prefer, stir the fruit into
the rice and serve the dessert in
individual dishes.

INGREDIENTS

Serves 4

65g/2½oz/5 tbsp short grain rice

900ml/1½ pint/3¾ cups semi-skimmed
   milk

1 cinnamon stick

175g/6oz/1 cup mixed dried fruit

175ml/6fl oz/¾ cup orange juice

45ml/3 tbsp caster sugar

finely grated rind of 1 small orange

1 Place the rice, milk and
cinnamon stick in a large pan
and bring to the boil. Cover and
simmer, stirring occasionally, for
about 1½ hours, until no free
liquid remains.

2 Meanwhile, place the fruit and
orange juice in a pan and
bring to the boil. Cover and
simmer very gently for about
1 hour, until tender and no free
liquid remains.

3 Remove the cinnamon stick
from the rice and stir in the
sugar and orange rind.

4 Tip the fruit into the base of a
lightly oiled 1.5 litre/2½ pint/
6¼ cup ring mould. Spoon the
rice over, smoothing down firmly.
Chill until needed.

5 Run a knife around the edge of
the mould and turn out the
rice carefully on to a serving plate.

Cherry Pancakes

These pancakes are virtually fat-free, and lower in calories and higher in fibre than traditional ones. Serve with a spoonful of natural yogurt or fromage frais.

Serves 4
50g/2oz/½ cup plain flour
50g/2oz/½ cup plain wholemeal flour
pinch of salt
1 egg white
150ml/¼ pint/⅔ cup skimmed milk
a little oil for frying

For the filling
425g/15oz can black cherries in juice
7.5ml/1½ tsp arrowroot

1 Sift the flours and salt into a bowl, adding any bran left in the sieve to the bowl at the end.

2 Make a well in the centre of the flour and add the egg white. Gradually beat in the milk and 150ml/¼ pint/⅔ cup of water, whisking hard until all the liquid is incorporated and the batter is smooth and bubbly.

3 Heat a non-stick pan with a small amount of oil until the pan is very hot. Pour in just enough batter to cover the base of the pan, swirling the pan to cover the base evenly.

4 Cook until the pancake is set and golden, and then turn to cook the other side. Remove to a sheet of absorbent paper and then cook the remaining batter to make about eight pancakes.

5 Drain the cherries, reserving the juice. Blend about 30ml/ 2 tbsp of the juice from the can of cherries with the arrowroot in a saucepan. Stir in the rest of the juice. Heat gently, stirring, until boiling. Stir over a moderate heat for about 2 minutes, until thickened and clear.

6 Add the cherries and stir until thoroughly heated. Spoon the cherries into the pancakes and fold them into quarters.

COOK'S TIP

The basic pancakes will freeze very successfully. Interleave them with non-stick or absorbent paper, wrap them in polythene and seal. Freeze for up to six months. Thaw at room temperature.

Apple Foam with Blackberries

This light dessert provides a good contrast in flavour, text and colour.

INGREDIENTS

Serves 4

225g/8oz blackberries
150ml/¼ pint/⅔ cup apple juice
5ml/1 tsp powdered gelatine
15ml/1 tbsp clear honey
2 egg whites

1 Place the blackberries in a pan with 60ml/4 tbsp of the apple juice and heat gently until the fruit is soft. Remove from the heat, cool and chill.

2 Sprinkle the gelatine over the remaining apple juice in another pan and stir over a low heat until dissolved. Stir in the honey.

3 Whisk the egg whites in a bowl until they hold stiff peaks. Continue whisking hard and pour in the hot gelatine mixture gradually, until well mixed.

4 Quickly spoon the foam into rough mounds on individual plates. Chill. Serve with the blackberries and juice spooned around.

VARIATION

Any seasonal soft fruit can be used to accompany the apple if blackberries are not available.

COOK'S TIP

Make sure that you dissolve the gelatine over a very low heat. It must not boil, or it will lose its setting ability.

Cappuccino Coffee Cups

Coffee-lovers will love this one – and it tastes rich and creamy, even though it's very light.

INGREDIENTS

Serves 4

2 eggs

215g/7.7oz carton evaporated semi-
   skimmed milk

25ml/1½ tbsp instant coffee granules
   or powder

30ml/2 tbsp caster sugar

10ml/2 tsp powdered gelatine,
   or alternative

60ml/4 tbsp light crème fraîche

cocoa powder or ground cinnamon,
   to decorate

1 Separate one egg and reserve
the white. Beat the yolk with
the whole of the remaining egg.

2 Put the evaporated milk,
coffee granules, sugar and
beaten eggs in a pan; whisk until
evenly combined.

3 Put the pan over a low heat and
stir constantly until the
mixture is hot, but not boiling.
Cook, stirring constantly, without
boiling, until the mixture is slightly
thickened and smooth.

4 Remove the pan from the
heat. Sprinkle the gelatine over
the pan and whisk until the
gelatine has completely dissolved.

5 Spoon the coffee custard into
four individual dishes or
glasses and chill them until set.

6 Whisk the reserved egg white
until stiff. Whisk in the crème
fraîche and then spoon the
mixture over the desserts. Sprinkle
with cocoa or cinnamon and serve.

VARIATION

Greek-style yogurt can be used
instead of the crème fraîche, if
you prefer.

Summer Fruit Salad Ice Cream

*What could be more cooling on a
hot day than fresh summer fruits,
lightly frozen in this irresistible ice?*

INGREDIENTS

Serves 6

900g/2lb/5 cups mixed soft summer fruit,
   such as raspberries, strawberries, blackcurrants, redcurrants, etc.
2 eggs
225g/8oz/1 cup Greek-style yogurt
175ml/6fl oz/¾ cup red grape juice
15ml/1 tbsp/1 sachet powdered gelatine,
   or alternative

1 Reserve half the fruit and purée
the rest in a blender or food
processor, or rub it through a sieve
to make a smooth purée.

2 Separate the eggs and whisk
the yolks and the yogurt into
the fruit purée.

3 Heat the grape juice until it's
almost boiling, then remove it
from the heat. Sprinkle the gelatine
over the juice and stir to dissolve
the gelatine completely.

4 Whisk the dissolved gelatine
mixture into the fruit purée
and then pour the mixture into a
freezer container. Freeze until half-
frozen and slushy in consistency.

5 Whisk the egg whites until they
are stiff. Quickly fold them into
the half-frozen mixture.

6 Return to the freezer and
freeze until almost firm. Scoop
into individual dishes or glasses
and add the reserved soft fruits.

Plum and Port Sorbet

Rather a grown-up sorbet, this one, but you could use fresh, still red grape juice in place of the port if you wished to leave out the alcohol.

INGREDIENTS

Serves 4–6

900g/2lb ripe red plums, halved
   and stoned
75g/3oz/6 tbsp caster sugar
45ml/3 tbsp ruby port or red wine
crisp biscuits, to serve (optional)

1 Place the plums in a pan with the sugar and 45ml/3 tbsp water. Stir over a low heat until the sugar is melted, then cover and simmer gently for about 5 minutes, until the fruit is soft.

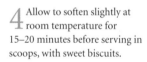

4 Allow to soften slightly at room temperature for 15–20 minutes before serving in scoops, with sweet biscuits.

2 Turn into a blender or food processor and purée until smooth, then stir in the port. Cool completely, then tip into a freezer container and freeze until firm round the edges.

3 Spoon into the food processor and process until smooth. Return to the freezer and freeze until solid.

Tofu Berry "Cheesecake"

This summery "cheesecake" is a very light and refreshing finish to any meal. Strictly speaking, it is not a cheesecake at all, as it's based on tofu – but who would guess?

INGREDIENTS

Serves 6

50g/2oz/4 tbsp low-fat spread

30ml/2 tbsp apple juice

115g/4oz/6 cups bran flakes or other high-fibre cereal

For the filling

275g/10oz/1¼ cups tofu or skimmed-milk soft cheese

200g/7oz/⅞ cup low-fat natural yogurt

15ml/1 tbsp/1 sachet powdered gelatine

60ml/4 tbsp apple juice

For the topping

175g/6oz/1¾ cups mixed summer soft fruit, e.g. strawberries, raspberries, red-currants, blackberries, etc. (or frozen "fruits of the forest")

30ml/2 tbsp redcurrant jelly

1 For the base, place the low-fat spread and apple juice in a pan and heat them gently until the spread has melted. Crush the cereal and stir it into the pan.

2 Tip into a 23cm/9in round flan tin and press down firmly. Leave to set.

3 For the filling, place the tofu or cheese and yogurt in a blender or food processor and process them until smooth. Dissolve the gelatine in the apple juice and stir the juice immediately into the tofu mixture.

4 Spread the tofu mixture over the chilled base, smoothing it evenly. Place in the fridge until the filling has set.

5 Remove the flan tin and place the "cheesecake" on a serving plate.

6 Arrange the fruits over the top. Melt the redcurrant jelly with 30ml/2 tbsp hot water. Let it cool, then spoon over the fruit to serve.

COOK'S TIP

The lowest-calorie breakfast cereals are usually those which are highest in fibre, so it is worth checking the labels for comparisons.

Floating Islands in Hot Plum Sauce

A low-fat version of the French
classic, that is simpler to make than
it looks. The plum sauce can be
made in advance, and reheated just
before you cook the meringues.

INGREDIENTS

Serves 4

450g/1lb red plums
300ml/½ pint/1¼ cups apple juice
2 egg whites
30ml/2 tbsp concentrated apple
    juice syrup
freshly grated nutmeg, to serve

1 Halve the plums and remove
the stones. Place them in a
wide pan, with the apple juice.

2 Bring to the boil and then
cover with a lid and leave to
simmer gently for 20–30 minutes
or until the plums are tender.

3 Place the egg whites in a clean,
dry bowl and whisk them
until they hold soft peaks.

4 Gradually whisk in the apple
juice syrup, whisking until the
meringue holds fairly firm peaks.

5 Using a tablespoon, scoop the
meringue mixture into the
gently simmering plum sauce. You
may need to cook the "islands" in
two batches.

COOK'S TIP
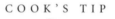

A bottle of concentrated apple
juice is a useful store cupboard
sweetener, but if you don't have
any, use a little honey instead.

6 Cover and allow to simmer
gently for 2–3 minutes, until
the meringues are just set. Serve
straight away, sprinkled with a
little freshly grated nutmeg.

Grilled Nectarines with Ricotta and Spice

This easy dessert is good at any time of year – use canned peach halves if fresh ones are not available.

INGREDIENTS

Serves 4

4 ripe nectarines or peaches

15ml/1 tbsp light muscovado sugar

115g/4oz/½ cup ricotta cheese or
 fromage frais

2.5ml/½ tsp ground star anise

1 Cut the nectarines in half and remove the stones.

2 Arrange the nectarines, cut-side upwards, in a wide flameproof dish or on a baking sheet.

COOK'S TIP

Star anise has a warm, rich flavour – if you can't get it, try ground cloves or ground mixed spice instead.

3 Stir the sugar into the ricotta or fromage frais. Using a teaspoon, spoon the mixture into the hollow of each nectarine half.

4 Sprinkle with the star anise. Place under a moderately hot grill for 6–8 minutes, or until the nectarines are hot and bubbling. Serve warm.

Chocolate Vanilla Timbales

*The occasional chocolate treat
doesn't do any harm, especially if it's
a dessert as light as this one.*

INGREDIENTS

Serves 6

350ml/12fl oz/1½ cups semi-skimmed
   milk
30ml/2 tbsp cocoa powder
2 eggs
5ml/1 tsp vanilla essence
45ml/3 tbsp caster sugar
15ml/1 tbsp/1 sachet powdered gelatine,
   or alternative
sprig of mint, to decorate

For the sauce
115g/4oz/½ cup light Greek-style yogurt
2.5ml/½ tsp vanilla essence
extra cocoa powder, to sprinkle

1 Place the milk and cocoa in a
saucepan and stir until the
milk is boiling. Separate the eggs
and beat the egg yolks with the
vanilla and sugar in a bowl, until
the mixture is pale and smooth.
Gradually pour in the chocolate
milk, beating well.

2 Return the mixture to the pan
and stir constantly over a
gentle heat, without boiling, until
it's slightly thickened and smooth.
Dissolve the gelatine in 45ml/
3 tbsp of hot water and then
quickly stir it into the milk
mixture. Let it cool until it's on the
point of setting.

3 Whisk the egg whites until
they hold soft peaks. Fold the
egg whites quickly into the milk
mixture. Spoon the timbale
mixture into six individual moulds
and chill them until set.

4 To serve, run a knife around
the edge, dip the moulds
quickly into hot water and turn
out the chocolate timbales on to
serving plates and decorate with a
sprig of mint. For the sauce, stir
together the yogurt and vanilla,
spoon on to the plates and sprinkle
with a little more cocoa powder.

Fluffy Banana and Pineapple Mousse

This light, low-fat mousse looks very impressive but is really very easy to make, especially with a food processor. To make it even simpler, use a 1 litre/1¾ pint/4 cup serving dish which will hold all the mixture without a paper "collar".

Serves 6

2 ripe bananas

225g/8oz/1 cup cottage cheese

425g/15oz can pineapple chunks or pieces
  in juice

15ml/1 tbsp/1 sachet powdered gelatine,
  or alternative

2 egg whites

1 Tie a double band of non-stick baking paper around a 600ml/1 pint/2½ cup soufflé dish, to come 5cm/2in above the rim.

2 Peel and chop one banana and place it in a blender or food processor with the cottage cheese. Process them until smooth.

3 Drain the pineapple, reserving the juice, and reserve a few pieces or chunks for decoration. Add the rest to the mixture in the blender or processor and process for a few seconds until finely chopped.

4 Dissolve the gelatine in 60ml/4 tbsp of the reserved pineapple juice. Stir the gelatine quickly into the fruit mixture.

5 Whisk the egg whites until they hold soft peaks and fold them into the mixture. Tip the mousse mixture into the prepared dish, smooth the surface and chill, until set.

6 When the mousse is set, carefully remove the paper collar and decorate with the reserved banana and pineapple.

Greek Honey and Lemon Cake

The semolina in this recipe gives the cake an excellent texture.

INGREDIENTS

Makes 16 slices

40g/1½oz/3 tbsp sunflower margarine
60ml/4 tbsp clear honey
finely grated rind and juice of 1 lemon
150ml/¼ pint/⅔ cup skimmed milk
150g/5oz/1¼ cups plain flour
7.5ml/1½ tsp baking powder
2.5ml/½ tsp grated nutmeg
50g/2oz/⅓ cup semolina
2 egg whites
10ml/2 tsp sesame seeds

1 Preheat the oven to 200°C/ 400°F/Gas 6. Lightly oil a 19cm/7½in square deep cake tin and line the base with non-stick baking paper.

2 Place the margarine and 45ml/3 tbsp of the honey in a saucepan and heat gently until melted. Reserve 15ml/1 tbsp lemon juice, then stir in the rest with the lemon rind and milk.

3 Stir together the flour, baking powder and nutmeg, then beat in with the semolina. Whisk the egg whites until they form soft peaks, then fold evenly into the semolina mixture.

4 Spoon into the tin and sprinkle with sesame seeds. Bake for 25–30 minutes, until golden brown.

5 Mix the reserved honey and lemon juice and drizzle over the cake while warm. Cool in the tin, then cut into fingers to serve.

Strawberry Roulade

An attractive and delicious cake, perfect for a family supper.

INGREDIENTS

Serves 6

4 egg whites
115g/4oz/scant ⅔ cup golden caster sugar
75g/3oz/⅔ cup plain flour, sifted
30ml/2 tbsp orange juice
caster sugar, for sprinkling
115g/4oz/1 cup strawberries, chopped
150g/5oz/¾ cup low-fat fromage frais
strawberries, to decorate

1 Preheat the oven to 200°C/ 400°F/Gas 6. Oil a 23 x 33cm/ 9 x 13in Swiss roll tin and line with non-stick baking paper.

2 Place the egg whites in a large clean bowl and whisk until they form soft peaks. Gradually whisk in the sugar. Fold in half of the sifted flour, then fold in the rest with the orange juice.

3 Spoon the mixture into the prepared tin, spreading evenly. Bake for 15–18 minutes, or until it is golden brown and firm to the touch.

4 Meanwhile, spread out a sheet of non-stick baking paper and sprinkle with caster sugar. Turn out the cake on to this and remove the lining paper. Roll up the sponge loosely from one short side, with the paper inside. Cool.

5 Unroll and remove the paper. Stir the strawberries into the fromage frais and spread over the sponge. Roll up and serve decorated with strawberries.

Apricot and Orange Roulade

*This elegant dessert is very good
served with a spoonful of Greek-
style yogurt or crème fraîche.*

· INGREDIENTS ·

Serves 6

4 egg whites

115g/4oz/scant ⅔ cup golden caster sugar

50g/2oz/½ cup plain flour

finely grated rind of 1 small orange

45ml/3 tbsp orange juice

For the filling

115g/4oz/½ cup ready-to-eat dried
   apricots

150ml/¼ pint/⅔ cup orange juice

10ml/2 tsp icing sugar, for sprinkling

shreds of orange zest, to decorate

1 Preheat the oven to
200°C/400°F/Gas 6. Grease a
23 x 33cm/9 x 13in Swiss roll tin
and line it with non-stick baking
paper. Grease the paper.

COOK'S TIP

Make and bake the sponge
mixture a day in advance and
keep it, rolled with the paper, in a
cool place. Fill it with the fruit
purée 2–3 hours before serving.
The sponge can also be frozen for
up to 2 months: thaw it at room
temperature and fill it as above.

2 To make the roulade, place the
egg whites in a large clean
bowl and whisk them until they
hold soft peaks. Gradually add the
sugar, whisking vigorously
between each addition.

3 Fold in the flour, orange rind
and juice. Spoon the mixture
into the prepared tin and spread
it evenly.

4 Bake for 15–18 minutes, or
until the sponge is firm and
light golden in colour. Turn out on
to a sheet of non-stick baking
paper and roll it up loosely from
one short side. Leave to cool.

5 Roughly chop the apricots and
place them in a pan, with the
orange juice. Cover the pan and
leave to simmer until most of the
liquid has been absorbed. Purée in
a blender or food processor.

6 Unroll the roulade and spread
with the apricot mixture. Roll
up, arrange strips of paper
diagonally across the roll, sprinkle
lightly with lines of icing sugar,
remove the paper and scatter with
orange zest to serve.

Filo Chiffon Pie

Filo pastry is low in fat and is very easy to use. Keep a pack in the freezer, ready to make impressive puddings like this one.

INGREDIENTS

Serves 3

500g/1¼lb pink rhubarb
5ml/1 tsp mixed spice
finely grated rind and juice of 1 orange
15ml/1 tbsp caster sugar
15g/½oz/1 tbsp butter
3 sheets filo pastry

1 Preheat the oven to 200°C/ 400°F/Gas 6. Trim the leaves and ends from the rhubarb sticks and chop them in 2.5cm/1in pieces. Place them in a bowl.

2 Add the mixed spice, orange rind and juice and sugar and toss well to coat evenly. Tip the rhubarb into a 1 litre/1¾ pint/ 4 cup pie dish.

3 Melt the butter and brush it over the pastry sheets. Lift the pastry sheets on to the pie dish, butter-side up, and crumple them to form a chiffon effect, covering the pie completely.

4 Place the dish on a baking sheet and bake it for 20 minutes, until golden brown. Reduce the heat to 180°C/350°F/ Gas 4 and bake for a further 10–15 minutes, until the rhubarb is tender. Serve warm.

VARIATION

Other fruit such as apples, pears or peaches can be used in this pie – try it with whatever is in season.

Crunchy Gooseberry Crumble

Gooseberries are perfect for traditional family puddings like this one. When they are out of season, other fruits such as apples, plums or rhubarb could be used instead.

INGREDIENTS

Serves 4

500g/1¼lb/5 cups gooseberries
50g/2oz/4 tbsp caster sugar
75g/3oz/scant 1 cup rolled oats
75g/3oz/⅔ cup wholemeal flour
60ml/4 tbsp sunflower oil
50g/2oz/4 tbsp demerara sugar
30ml/2 tbsp chopped walnuts
natural yogurt or custard, to serve

1 Preheat the oven to 200°C/ 400°F/Gas 6. Place the gooseberries in a pan with the caster sugar. Cover the pan and cook over a low heat for 10 minutes, until the gooseberries are just tender. Tip into an ovenproof dish.

2 To make the crumble, place the oats, flour and oil in a bowl and stir with a fork until evenly mixed.

3 Stir in the demerara sugar and walnuts, then spread evenly over the gooseberries. Bake for 25–30 minutes, or until golden and bubbling. Serve hot with yogurt, or custard made with skimmed milk.

COOK'S TIP

The best gooseberries to use for cooking are the early, small, firm green ones.

Spiced Date and Walnut Cake

A classic flavour combination, which makes a very easy low fat, high-fibre cake.

INGREDIENTS

Makes 1 cake

300g/11oz/2¾ cups wholemeal self-raising
   flour
10ml/2 tsp mixed spice
150g/5oz/1 cup chopped dates
50g/2oz/½ cup chopped walnuts
60ml/4 tbsp sunflower oil
115g/4oz/½ cup dark muscovado sugar
300ml/½ pint/1¼ cups skimmed milk
walnut halves, to decorate

1 Preheat the oven to 180°C/
350°F/Gas 4. Grease and line
a 900g/2lb loaf tin with greaseproof paper.

2 Sift together the flour and
spice, adding back any bran
from the sieve. Stir in the dates
and walnuts.

3 Mix the oil, sugar and milk,
then stir evenly into the dry
ingredients. Spoon into the
prepared tin and arrange the
walnut halves on top.

4 Bake the cake in the oven for
about 45–50 minutes, or until
golden brown and firm. Turn out
the cake, remove the lining paper
and leave to cool on a wire rack.

VARIATION

Pecan nuts can be used in place of
the walnuts in this cake.

Banana Orange Loaf

For the best banana flavour and a really good, moist texture, make sure the bananas are very ripe.

INGREDIENTS

Makes 1 loaf

90g/3½oz/generous ¾ cup wholemeal plain flour

90g/3½oz/generous ¾ cup plain flour

5ml/1 tsp baking powder

5ml/1 tsp ground mixed spice

45ml/3 tbsp flaked hazelnuts, toasted

2 large ripe bananas

1 egg

30ml/2 tbsp sunflower oil

30ml/2 tbsp clear honey

finely grated rind and juice of 1 small orange

4 orange slices, halved

10ml/2 tsp icing sugar

1 Preheat the oven to 180°C/ 350°F/Gas 4. Brush a 1 litre/ 1¾ pint/4 cup loaf tin with sunflower oil and line the base with non-stick baking paper.

2 Sift the flours with the baking powder and spice into a bowl.

3 Stir the hazelnuts into the dry ingredients. Peel and mash the bananas. Beat in the egg, oil, honey and the orange rind and juice. Stir evenly into the dry ingredients.

4 Spoon into the prepared tin and smooth the top. Bake for 40–45 minutes, or until firm and golden brown. Turn out and cool on a wire rack.

5 Sprinkle the orange slices with the icing sugar and grill until golden. Use to decorate the cake.

COOK'S TIP

If you plan to keep the loaf for more than two or three days, omit the orange slices. Brush the cake with honey and sprinkle with flaked hazelnuts.

Banana Ginger Parkin

Parkin improves with keeping. Store it in a covered container for up to two months.

INGREDIENTS

Makes 12 squares

200g/7oz/1¾ cups plain flour
10ml/2 tsp bicarbonate of soda
10ml/2 tsp ground ginger
150g/5oz/1¼ cups medium oatmeal
60ml/4 tbsp dark muscovado sugar
75g/3oz/6 tbsp sunflower margarine
150g/5oz/⅔ cup golden syrup
1 egg, beaten
3 ripe bananas, mashed
75g/3oz/¾ cup icing sugar
stem ginger, to decorate

1 Preheat the oven to 160°C/325°F/Gas 3. Grease and line an 18 x 28cm/7 x 11in cake tin.

2 Sift together the flour, bicarbonate of soda and ginger, then stir in the oatmeal. Melt the sugar, margarine and syrup in a saucepan, then stir into the flour mixture. Beat in the egg and mashed bananas.

3 Spoon into the tin and bake for about 1 hour, or until firm to the touch. Allow to cool in the tin, then turn out and cut into even-sized squares.

4 Sift the icing sugar into a bowl and stir in just enough water to make a smooth, runny icing. Drizzle the icing over each square and top with pieces of stem ginger, if you like.

COOK'S TIP
∾
This is a nutritious cake, ideal for packed lunches as it doesn't break up too easily.

FRUIT
DESSERTS

~

Cherries Jubilee

Fresh cherries are wonderful cooked lightly to serve hot over ice cream. Children will love this dessert.

Serves 4

450g/1lb red or black cherries
115g/4oz/generous ½ cup granulated
   sugar
pared rind of 1 lemon
15ml/1 tbsp arrowroot
60ml/4 tbsp Kirsch
vanilla ice cream, to serve

COOK'S TIP

If you don't have a cherry stoner, simply push the stones through with a skewer. Remember to save the juice to use in the recipe.

1 Stone the cherries over a pan to catch the juice. Drop the stones into the pan as you work.

2 Add the sugar, lemon rind and 300ml/½ pint/1¼ cups water to the pan. Stir over a low heat until the sugar dissolves, then bring to the boil and simmer for 10 minutes. Strain the syrup, then return to the pan. Add the cherries and cook for 3–4 minutes.

3 Blend the arrowroot to a paste with 15ml/1 tbsp cold water and stir into the cherries, after removing them from the heat.

4 Return the pan to the heat and bring to the boil, stirring all the time. Cook the sauce for a minute or two, stirring until it is thick and smooth. Heat the Kirsch in a ladle over a flame, ignite and pour over the cherries. Spoon the cherries and hot sauce over scoops of ice cream and serve at once.

Apricots in Marsala

Make sure the apricots are completely covered by the syrup so that they don't discolour.

Serves 4

12 apricots
50g/2oz/4 tbsp caster sugar
300ml/½ pint/1¼ cups Marsala
2 strips pared orange rind
1 vanilla pod, split
150ml/¼ pint/⅔ cup double or whipping
   cream
15ml/1 tbsp icing sugar
1.5ml/¼ tsp ground cinnamon
150ml/¼ pint/⅔ cup Greek-style yogurt

1 Halve and stone the apricots, then place in a bowl of boiling water for about 30 seconds. Drain well, then slip off their skins.

2 Place the caster sugar, Marsala, orange rind, vanilla pod and 250ml/8fl oz/1 cup water in a pan. Heat gently until the sugar dissolves. Bring to the boil, without stirring, then simmer for 2–3 minutes.

3 Add the apricot halves to the pan and poach for 5–6 minutes, or until just tender. Using a slotted spoon, transfer the apricots to a serving dish.

4 Boil the syrup rapidly until reduced by half, then pour over the apricots and leave to cool. Cover and chill. Remove the orange rind and vanilla pod.

5 Whip the cream with the icing sugar and cinnamon until it forms soft peaks. Gently fold in the yogurt. Spoon into a serving bowl and chill. Serve with the apricots.

Poached Pears in Red Wine

This makes a very pretty dessert, as the pears take on a red blush from the wine.

INGREDIENTS

Serves 4

1 bottle red wine

150g/5oz/¾ cup caster sugar

45ml/3 tbsp honey

juice of ½ lemon

1 cinnamon stick

1 vanilla pod, split open lengthways

5cm/2in piece of orange rind

1 clove

1 black peppercorn

4 firm, ripe pears

whipped cream or soured cream, to serve

1 Place the wine, sugar, honey, lemon juice, cinnamon stick, vanilla pod, orange rind, clove and peppercorn in a saucepan just large enough to hold the pears standing upright. Heat gently, stirring occasionally until the sugar has completely dissolved.

2 Meanwhile, peel the pears, leaving the stem intact. Take a thin slice off the base of each pear so that it will stand square and upright in the pan.

3 Place the pears in the wine mixture, then simmer, uncovered, for 20–35 minutes depending on size and ripeness, until the pears are just tender; be careful not to overcook.

4 Carefully transfer the pears to a bowl using a slotted spoon. Continue to boil the poaching liquid until reduced by about half. Leave to cool, then strain the cooled liquid over the pears and chill for at least 3 hours.

5 Place the pears in four individual serving dishes and spoon over a little of the red wine syrup. Serve with whipped cream or soured cream.

Hot Bananas with Rum and Raisins

Choose almost-ripe bananas with evenly coloured skins, either all yellow or just green at the tips. Over-ripe bananas will not hold their shape so well when cooked.

INGREDIENTS

Serves 4

40g/1½oz/scant ¼ cup seedless raisins

75ml/5 tbsp dark rum

50g/2oz/4 tbsp unsalted butter

60ml/4 tbsp soft light brown sugar

4 ripe bananas, peeled and halved
lengthways

1.5ml/¼ tsp grated nutmeg

1.5ml/¼ tsp ground cinnamon

30ml/2 tbsp slivered almonds, toasted

chilled cream or vanilla ice cream, to serve
(optional)

1 Put the raisins in a bowl with the rum. Leave them to soak for about 30 minutes to plump up.

2 Melt the butter in a frying pan, add the sugar and stir until dissolved. Add the bananas and cook for a few minutes until they are tender.

3 Sprinkle the spices over the bananas, then pour in the rum and raisins. Carefully set alight using a long taper and stir gently to mix.

4 Scatter over the slivered almonds and serve immediately with chilled cream or vanilla ice cream, if you like.

Blueberry Pancakes

These are rather like the thick American breakfast pancakes – though they can, of course, be eaten at any time of the day.

INGREDIENTS

Makes 6–8

115g/4oz/1 cup self-raising flour
pinch of salt
45–60ml/3–4 tbsp caster sugar
2 eggs
120ml/4fl oz/½ cup milk
15–30ml/1–2 tbsp oil
115g/4oz/1 cup fresh or frozen
    blueberries, plus extra to decorate
maple syrup, to serve
lemon wedges, to decorate

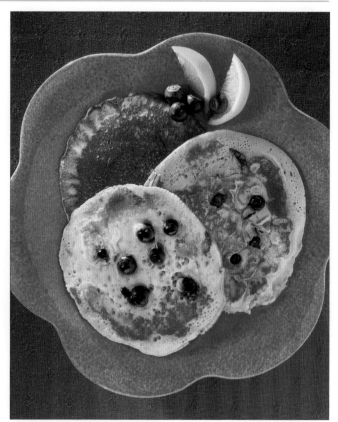

1 Sift the flour into a bowl with the salt and sugar. Beat together the eggs thoroughly. Make a well in the middle of the flour and stir in the eggs.

2 Gradually blend in a little of the milk to make a smooth batter. Then whisk in the rest of the milk and whisk for 1–2 minutes. Allow to rest for 20–30 minutes.

COOK'S TIP

Instead of blueberries you could use blackberries or raspberries. If you use canned fruit, make sure it is very well drained.

3 Heat a few drops of oil in a pancake pan or heavy-based frying pan until just hazy. Pour about 30ml/2 tbsp of the batter and swirl the batter around until it makes an even shape.

4 Cook for 2–3 minutes and when almost set on top, sprinkle over 15–30ml/1–2 tbsp blueberries. As soon as the base is loose and golden brown, turn the pancake over.

5 Cook on the second side for only about 1 minute, until golden and crisp. Slide the pancake on to a plate and serve drizzled with maple syrup. Continue with the rest of the batter. Serve decorated with lemon wedges and a few extra blueberries.

Rhubarb-Strawberry Crisp

Strawberries, cinnamon and ground almonds make this a luxurious and delicious version of rhubarb crumble.

INGREDIENTS

Serves 4

225g/8oz strawberries, hulled

450g/1lb rhubarb, diced

90g/3½oz/½ cup granulated sugar

15ml/1 tbsp cornflour

85ml/3fl oz/⅓ cup fresh orange juice

115g/4oz/1 cup plain flour

90g/3½oz/1 cup rolled oats

115g/4oz/½ cup light brown sugar, firmly packed

2.5ml/½ tsp ground cinnamon

50g/2oz/½ cup ground almonds

150g/5oz/generous ½ cup cold butter

1 egg, lightly beaten

1 If the strawberries are large, cut them in half. Combine the strawberries, rhubarb and granulated sugar in a 2.4 litre/ 4 pint/10 cup baking dish. Preheat the oven to 180°C/350°F/Gas 4.

2 In a small bowl, blend the cornflour with the orange juice. Pour this mixture over the fruit and stir gently to coat. Set the baking dish aside while making the crumble topping.

3 In a bowl, toss together the flour, oats, brown sugar, cinnamon and ground almonds. With a pastry blender or two knives, cut in the butter until the mixture resembles coarse bread-crumbs. Stir in the beaten egg.

4 Spoon the oat mixture evenly over the fruit and press down gently. Bake until browned, 50–60 minutes, then serve warm.

Fruit Kebabs with Mango and Yogurt Sauce

These mixed fresh fruit kebabs make an attractive and healthy dessert.

INGREDIENTS

Serves 4

½ pineapple, peeled, cored and cubed

2 kiwi fruit, peeled and cubed

175g/6oz/1½ cups strawberries, hulled
and cut in half, if large

½ mango, peeled, stoned and cubed

For the sauce

120ml/4fl oz/½ cup fresh mango purée,
from 1–1½ peeled and pitted mangoes

120ml/4fl oz/½ cup thick plain yogurt

5ml/1 tsp caster sugar

few drops vanilla essence

15ml/1 tbsp finely chopped mint leaves

1 To make the sauce, beat
together the mango purée,
yogurt, sugar and vanilla with an
electric mixer.

2 Stir in the chopped mint.
Cover the sauce and place in
the fridge until required.

3 Thread the prepared fruit
on to twelve 15cm/6in wooden
skewers, alternating the pineapple,
kiwi fruit, strawberries and
mango cubes.

4 Arrange the kebabs on a large
serving tray with the mango
and yogurt sauce in the centre.

Tropical Fruits in Cinnamon Syrup

*An exotic glazed fruit salad, a
simply prepared but satisfying end
to any meal.*

INGREDIENTS

Serves 6

450g/1lb/2¼ cups caster sugar

1 cinnamon stick

1 large or 2 medium paw paws (about
675g/1½lb), peeled, seeded and cut
lengthways into thin pieces

1 large or 2 medium mangoes (about
675g/1½lb), peeled, stoned and cut
lengthways into thin pieces

1 large or 2 small star fruit (about
225g/8oz), thinly sliced

yogurt or crème fraîche, to serve

1 Sprinkle one-third of the sugar
over the base of a large
saucepan. Add the cinnamon stick
and half the paw paw, mango and
star fruit pieces.

2 Sprinkle half of the remaining
sugar over the fruit pieces in
the pan. Add all the remaining
fruit and sprinkle with the rest of
the sugar.

3 Cover the pan and cook the
fruit over a medium-low heat
for 35–45 minutes, until the sugar
melts completely. Shake the pan
occasionally, but do not stir or the
fruit will collapse.

4 Uncover the pan and simmer
until the fruit begins to appear
translucent, about 10 minutes.
Remove the pan from the heat and
leave to cool.

5 Transfer the fruit and syrup to
a bowl, cover and chill
overnight. Serve with yogurt or
crème fraîche.

Mango Sorbet

A light and refreshing dessert that's surprisingly easy to make.

INGREDIENTS

Serves 6

150g/5oz/¾ cup caster sugar

a large strip of orange rind

1 large mango, peeled, stoned and cubed

60ml/4 tbsp orange juice

mint sprigs, to decorate

1 Combine the sugar, orange rind and 175ml/6fl oz/¾ cup of water in a saucepan. Bring to the boil, stirring to dissolve the sugar. Leave the syrup to cool.

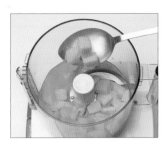

2 Purée the mango cubes with the orange juice in a blender or food processor. There should be about 475ml/16fl oz/2 cups of purée.

3 Add the purée to the cooled sugar syrup and mix well. Strain, then chill.

4 When cold, tip into a freezer container and freeze until firm around the edges.

5 Spoon the semi-frozen mixture into the food processor and process until smooth. Return to the freezer and freeze until solid. Allow the sorbet to soften slightly at room temperature for 15–20 minutes before serving, decorated with mint sprigs.

VARIATIONS

For Banana Sorbet: peel and cube 4–5 large bananas. Purée with 30ml/2 tbsp lemon juice to make 475ml/16fl oz/2 cups. If liked, replace the orange rind in the sugar syrup with 2–3 whole cloves, or omit the rind.

For Paw Paw Sorbet: peel, seed and cube 675g/1½lb paw paw. Purée with 45ml/3 tbsp lime juice to make 475ml/16fl oz/2 cups. Replace the orange rind with lime rind.

For Passion Fruit Sorbet: halve 16 or more passion fruit and scoop out the seeds and pulp (there should be about 475ml/16fl oz/ 2 cups). Work in a blender or food processor until the seeds are like coarse pepper. Omit the orange juice and rind. Add the passion fruit to the sugar syrup, then press through a wire sieve before freezing.

Raspberry Trifle

Use fresh or frozen raspberries for this ever-popular dessert.

Serves 6 or more

175g/6oz trifle sponges, or 2.5cm/1in
  cubes of plain Victoria sponge or
  coarsely crumbled sponge fingers
60ml/4 tbsp medium sherry
115g/4oz raspberry jam
275g/10oz/1⅔ cups raspberries
450ml/¾ pint/scant 2 cups custard,
  flavoured with 30ml/2 tbsp medium or
  sweet sherry
300ml/½ pint/1¼ cups sweetened
  whipped cream
toasted flaked almonds and mint leaves,
  to decorate

1 Spread half of the sponges,
cake cubes or sponge fingers
over the bottom of a large serving
bowl. (A glass bowl is best for
presentation.)

2 Sprinkle half of the sherry over
the cake to moisten it. Spoon
over half of the jam, dotting it
evenly over the cake cubes.

3 Reserve a few raspberries for
decoration. Make a layer of
half of the remaining raspberries
on top.

4 Pour over half of the custard,
covering the fruit and cake.
Repeat the layers. Cover and chill
for at least 2 hours.

5 Before serving, spoon the
sweetened whipped cream
evenly over the top. To decorate,
sprinkle with toasted flaked
almonds and arrange the reserved
raspberries and the mint leaves on
the top.

VARIATION

Use other ripe summer fruit such
as apricots, peaches, nectarines and
strawberries in the trifle, with jam
and liqueur to suit.

Apple Fritters

Make sure you buy plenty of apples for this recipe. They taste so good you'll probably have to cook an extra batch.

INGREDIENTS

Serves 4–6

130g/4½oz/1⅓ cups plain flour

10ml/2 tsp baking powder

1.5ml/¼ tsp salt

150ml/¼ pint/⅔ cup milk

1 egg, beaten

oil for deep-frying

150g/5oz/¾ cup granulated sugar

5ml/1 tsp ground cinnamon

2 large tart-sweet apples, peeled, cored,
    and cut in 5mm/¼ in slices

icing sugar, for dusting

1 Sift the flour, baking powder and salt into a bowl. Beat in the milk and egg with a wire whisk.

2 Heat at least 7.5cm/3in oil in a heavy frying pan to 185°C/360°F or until a cube of bread browns in 1–2 minutes.

3 Mix the granulated sugar and cinnamon in a shallow bowl or plate. Toss the apple slices in the sugar mixture to coat all over.

4 Dip the apple slices in the batter, using a fork or slotted spoon. Drain off excess batter. Fry, in batches, in the hot oil until golden brown on both sides, about 4–5 minutes. Drain the fritters on kitchen paper.

5 Sprinkle with icing sugar, and serve hot.

Cherry Compote

Sweet cherries in syrup to serve with cream or ice cream.

INGREDIENTS

Serves 6

120ml/4fl oz/½ cup red wine

50g/2oz/¼ cup light brown sugar,
    firmly packed

50g/2oz/¼ cup granulated sugar

15ml/1 tbsp honey

2 2.5cm/1in strips of orange rind

1.5ml/¼ tsp almond extract

675g/1½lb sweet fresh cherries, pitted

ice cream or whipped cream, for serving

1 Combine all the ingredients except the cherries and ice cream or whipped cream in a saucepan with 120ml/4fl oz/½ cup water. Stir over medium heat until the sugar dissolves. Raise the heat and boil until the liquid reduces slightly.

2 Add the cherries. Bring back to the boil. Reduce the heat slightly and simmer for 8–10 minutes. If necessary, skim off any foam.

3 Let cool to lukewarm. Spoon warm over vanilla ice cream, or refrigerate and serve cold with whipped cream, if desired.

Clementines in Cinnamon Caramel

The combination of sweet, yet sharp
clementines and caramel sauce with
a hint of spice is divine. Served with
Greek-style yogurt or crème fraîche,
this makes a delicious dessert.

INGREDIENTS

Serves 4–6

8–12 clementines

225g/8oz/generous 1 cup granulated sugar

2 cinnamon sticks

30ml/2 tbsp orange-flavoured liqueur

25g/1oz/¼ cup shelled pistachio nuts

1 Pare the rind from two
clementines using a vegetable
peeler and cut it into fine strips.
Set aside.

2 Peel the clementines, removing
all the pith but keeping them
intact. Put the fruits in a serving
bowl.

3 Gently heat the sugar in a pan
until it melts and turns a rich
golden brown. Immediately turn
off the heat.

4 Cover your hand with a dish
towel and pour in 300ml/
½ pint/1¼ cups warm water (the
mixture will bubble and splutter).
Bring slowly to the boil, stirring
until the caramel has dissolved.
Add the shredded peel and
cinnamon sticks, then simmer for
5 minutes. Stir in the orange-
flavoured liqueur.

5 Leave the syrup to cool for
about 10 minutes, then pour
over the clementines. Cover the
bowl and chill for several hours
or overnight.

6 Blanch the pistachio nuts in
boiling water. Drain, cool and
remove the dark outer skins.
Scatter over the clementines and
serve at once.

Chocolate Amaretti Peaches

Quick and easy to prepare, this delicious dessert can also be made with fresh nectarines or apricots.

INGREDIENTS

Serves 4

115g/4oz amaretti biscuits, crushed

50g/2oz plain chocolate, chopped

grated rind of ½ orange

15ml/1 tbsp clear honey

1.5ml/¼ tsp ground cinnamon

1 egg white, lightly beaten

4 firm ripe peaches

150ml/¼ pint/⅔ cup white wine

15ml/1 tbsp caster sugar

whipped cream, to serve

1 Preheat the oven to 190°C/375°F/Gas 5. Mix together the crushed amaretti biscuits, chocolate, orange rind, honey and cinnamon in a bowl. Add the beaten egg white and mix to bind the mixture together.

2 Halve and stone the peaches and fill the cavities with the chocolate mixture, mounding it up slightly.

3 Arrange the stuffed peaches in a lightly buttered, shallow ovenproof dish which will just hold the peaches comfortably. Pour the wine into a measuring cup and stir in the sugar.

4 Pour the wine mixture around the peaches. Bake for 30–40 minutes, until the peaches are tender. Serve at once with a little of the cooking juices spooned over and the whipped cream.

Fruity Ricotta Creams

Ricotta is an Italian soft cheese with a smooth texture and a mild, slightly sweet flavour. Served here with candied fruit peel and delicious chocolate – it is quite irresistible.

INGREDIENTS

Serves 4

350g/12oz/1½ cups ricotta cheese

30–45ml/2–3 tbsp Cointreau or other
    orange liqueur

10ml/2 tsp grated lemon rind

30ml/2 tbsp icing sugar

150ml/¼ pint/⅔ cup double cream

150g/5oz/scant 1 cup candied peel, such as
    orange, lemon and citron, finely
    chopped

50g/2oz plain chocolate, finely chopped

chocolate curls, to decorate

amaretti biscuits, to serve (optional)

1 Using the back of a wooden spoon, push the ricotta through a fine sieve into a large bowl.

2 Add the liqueur, lemon rind and icing sugar to the ricotta and beat well until the mixture is light and smooth.

3 Whip the cream in a large bowl until it forms soft peaks.

4 Gently fold the cream into the ricotta mixture with the candied peel and chopped chocolate.

5 Spoon the mixture into four glass serving dishes and chill for about 1 hour. Decorate the ricotta creams with chocolate curls and serve with amaretti biscuits, if you like.

Hot Fruit with Maple Butter

Turn exotic fruits into comfort food by grilling them with maple syrup and butter.

INGREDIENTS

Serves 4

1 large mango

1 large paw paw

1 small pineapple

2 bananas

115g/4oz/½ cup unsalted butter

60ml/4 tbsp pure maple syrup

ground cinnamon, for sprinkling

COOK'S TIP
∽

Prepare the fruit just before grilling to prevent it discolouring.

1 Peel the mango and cut the flesh into large pieces. Halve the paw paw and scoop out the seeds. Cut into thick slices, then peel away the skin.

2 Peel and core the pineapple and slice into thin wedges. Peel the bananas then halve them lengthways.

3 Cut the butter into small dice and place in a blender or food processor with the maple syrup, then process until the mixture is smooth and creamy.

4 Place the mango, paw paw, pineapple and banana on a grill rack and brush with the maple syrup butter.

5 Cook the fruit under a medium heat for about 10 minutes, until just tender, turning the fruit occasionally and brushing it with the butter.

6 Arrange the fruit on a warmed serving platter and dot with the remaining butter. Sprinkle over a little ground cinnamon and serve the fruit piping hot.

Ruby Fruit Salad

After a rich main course, this port-flavoured fruit salad is light and refreshing. Use any combination of fruit that is available.

Serves 8

115g/4oz/8 tbsp caster sugar

1 cinnamon stick

4 cloves

pared rind of 1 orange

300ml/½ pint/1¼ cups port

2 oranges

1 small ripe Ogen, Charentais or
    honeydew melon

4 small bananas

2 dessert apples

225g/8oz seedless grapes

1 Put the sugar, spices, pared orange rind and 300ml/½ pint/1¼ cups of water into a pan and stir over a gentle heat to dissolve the sugar. Then bring to the boil, cover with a lid and simmer for 10 minutes. Leave to cool, then add the port.

2 Strain the liquid (to remove the spices and orange rind) into a bowl. With a sharp knife, cut off all the skin and pith from the oranges. Then, holding each orange over the bowl to catch the juice, cut away the segments, by slicing between the membrane that divides each segment and allowing the segments to drop into the syrup. Squeeze the remaining pith to release any juice.

3 Cut the melon in half, remove the seeds and scoop out the flesh with a melon baller, or cut it in small cubes. Add it to the syrup.

4 Peel the bananas and cut them diagonally in 1cm/½in slices. Quarter and core the apples and cut them in small cubes. Leave the skin on, or peel them if it is tough. Halve the grapes if large or leave them whole. Stir all the fruit into the syrup, cover with clear film and chill for 1 hour before serving.

Summer Pudding

Unbelievably simple to make and totally delicious, this is a real warm weather classic.

INGREDIENTS

Serves 4

about 8 thin slices day-old white bread,
    crusts removed
800g/1¾lb mixed summer fruits
about 30ml/2 tbsp granulated sugar

1 Cut a round from one slice of bread to fit in the base of a 1.2 litre/2 pint/5 cup pudding basin, then cut strips of bread about 5cm/2in wide to line the basin, overlapping the strips.

2 Gently heat the fruit, sugar and 30ml/2 tbsp water in a large heavy saucepan, shaking the pan occasionally, until the juices begin to run.

3 Reserve about 45ml/3 tbsp fruit juice, then spoon the fruit and remaining juice into the basin, taking care not to dislodge the bread lining.

4 Cut the remaining bread to fit entirely over the fruit. Stand the basin on a plate and cover with a saucer or small plate that will just fit inside the top of the basin. Place a heavy weight on top. Chill the pudding and the reserved fruit juice overnight.

5 Run a knife carefully around the inside of the basin rim, then invert the pudding on to a cold serving plate. Pour over the reserved juice and serve.

COOK'S TIP

Summer pudding freezes well so make an extra one to enjoy during the winter.

Banana Honey Yogurt Ice

Using yogurt instead of cream gives this cool dessert a more refreshing, less sugary taste.

INGREDIENTS

Serves 4–6

4 ripe bananas, roughly chopped

15ml/1 tbsp lemon juice

30ml/2 tbsp clear honey

250g/9oz/generous 1 cup Greek-style
   yogurt

2.5ml/½ tsp ground cinnamon

crisp biscuits, flaked hazelnuts and
   banana slices, to serve

1 Place the bananas in a food processor or blender with the lemon juice, honey, yogurt and cinnamon. Process until smooth and creamy.

2 Pour the mixture into a freezer container and freeze until almost solid. Spoon back into the food processor and process again until smooth.

3 Pour back into the freezer container and freeze until firm. Allow to soften at room temperature for 15 minutes, then serve, with crisp biscuits, flaked hazelnuts and banana slices.

VARIATION

To make Banana Maple Yogurt Ice, use maple syrup in place of honey.

Autumn Pudding

As its name suggests, this is a tasty seasonal variation of summer pudding using apples, blackberries and plums.

INGREDIENTS

Serves 6

10 slices white or brown bread, at least
   one day old

1 Bramley cooking apple, peeled, cored
   and sliced

225g/8oz ripe red plums, halved and
   stoned

225g/8oz blackberries

75g/3oz/6 tbsp caster sugar

low fat yogurt or fromage frais, to serve

1 Remove the crusts from the bread and use a biscuit cutter to stamp out a 7.5cm/3in round from one slice. Cut the remaining slices in half.

2 Place the bread round the base of a 1.2 litre/2 pint/5 cup pudding basin, then overlap the fingers around the sides, saving some for the top.

3 Place the apple, plums, black-berries, caster sugar and 60ml/4 tbsp of water in a pan, heat gently until the sugar dissolves, then simmer for 10 minutes, until soft. Remove from the heat.

4 Reserve the juice and spoon the fruit into the bread-lined basin. Top with the reserved bread, then gently spoon over the reserved fruit juices.

5 Cover the mould with a saucer and place weights on top. Chill the pudding overnight. Turn out on to a serving plate and serve with low fat yogurt or fromage frais.

COOK'S TIP

Choose good quality bread that is not too thinly sliced – it needs to be at least 5mm/¼in thick so that it supports the fruit when the pudding is turned out.

Ruby Plum Mousse

Red plums and port give this mousse
its delicate flavour and colour.

INGREDIENTS

Serves 6

450g/1lb ripe red plums

45ml/3 tbsp granulated sugar

60ml/4 tbsp ruby port

15ml/1 tbsp/1 sachet powdered gelatine

3 eggs, separated

115g/4oz/generous ½ cup caster sugar

150ml/¼ pint/⅔ cup double cream

skinned and chopped pistachio nuts, to
  decorate

cinnamon biscuits, to serve (optional)

1 Place the plums and granulated
sugar in a pan with 30ml/
2 tbsp water. Cook over a low heat
until softened. Press the fruit
through a sieve to remove the
stones and skins. Leave to cool,
then stir in the port.

2 Put 45ml/3 tbsp water in a
small bowl, sprinkle over the
gelatine and leave to soften. Stand
the bowl in a pan of hot water and
leave until dissolved. Stir into the
plum purée.

3 Place the egg yolks and caster
sugar in a bowl and whisk
until thick and mousse-like. Fold
in the plum purée, then whip the
cream and fold in gently.

4 Whisk the egg whites until
they hold stiff peaks, then
carefully fold in using a metal
spoon. Divide among six glasses
and chill until set.

5 Decorate the mousses with
chopped pistachio nuts and
serve with crisp cinnamon
biscuits, if liked.

Warm Autumn Compote

An easily prepared dessert with a
sophisticated taste.

INGREDIENTS

Serves 4

75g/3oz/6 tbsp caster sugar

1 bottle red wine

1 vanilla pod, split

1 strip pared lemon rind

4 pears

2 purple figs, quartered

225g/8oz/1⅓ cups raspberries

lemon juice, to taste

1 Put the sugar and wine in a
large pan and heat gently until
the sugar is dissolved. Add the
vanilla pod and lemon rind and
bring to the boil, then simmer for
5 minutes.

2 Peel and halve the pears, then
scoop out the cores, using a
melon baller. Add the pears to the
syrup and poach for 15 minutes,
turning the pears several times so
they colour evenly.

3 Add the figs and poach for a
further 5 minutes, until the
fruits are tender.

4 Transfer the poached pears
and figs to a serving bowl
using a slotted spoon, then scatter
over the raspberries.

5 Return the syrup to the heat
and boil rapidly to reduce
slightly and concentrate the
flavour. Add a little lemon juice to
taste. Strain the syrup over the
fruits and serve warm.

Apricot and Pear Filo Roulade

This is a very quick way of making a strudel – normally, very time consuming to do – it tastes delicious all the same!

INGREDIENTS

Serves 4–6

115g/4oz/½ cup ready-to-eat dried
   apricots, chopped
30ml/2 tbsp apricot jam
5ml/1 tsp lemon juice
50g/2oz/¼ cup soft brown sugar
2 medium pears, peeled, cored
   and chopped
50g/2oz/½ cup ground almonds
30ml/2 tbsp slivered almonds
25g/1oz/2 tbsp butter
8 sheets filo pastry
icing sugar, to dust

1 Put the apricots, apricot jam, lemon juice, brown sugar and pears into a pan and heat gently, stirring, for 5–7 minutes.

2 Remove from the heat and cool. Mix in the ground and slivered almonds. Preheat the oven to 200°C/400°F/Gas 6. Melt the butter in a pan.

3 Lightly grease a baking sheet. Layer the pastry on the baking sheet, brushing each layer with the melted butter.

4 Spoon the filling down the pastry just to one side of the centre and within 2.5cm/1in of each end. Lift the other side of the pastry up by sliding a palette knife underneath.

5 Fold this pastry over the filling, tucking the edge under. Seal the ends neatly and brush all over with butter again.

6 Bake for 15–20 minutes, until golden. Dust with icing sugar and serve hot.

Red Berry Tart with Lemon Cream Filling

This flan is best filled just before serving so the pastry remains mouth-wateringly crisp. Select red berry fruits such as strawberries, raspberries or redcurrants.

INGREDIENTS

Serves 6–8

150g/5oz/1¼ cups plain flour
25g/1oz/¼ cup cornflour
40g/1½oz/5 tbsp icing sugar
90g/3½oz/7 tbsp butter
5ml/1 tsp vanilla essence
2 egg yolks, beaten
sprig of mint, to decorate

For the filling

200g/7oz/scant 1 cup cream cheese
45ml/3 tbsp lemon curd
grated rind and juice of 1 lemon
icing sugar, to sweeten (optional)
225g/8oz/2 cups mixed red berry fruits
45ml/3 tbsp redcurrant jelly

1 Sift the flour, cornflour and icing sugar together, then rub in the butter until the mixture resembles breadcrumbs.

2 Beat the vanilla into the egg yolks, then mix into the crumbs to make a firm dough, adding cold water if necessary.

3 Roll out and line a 23cm/9in round flan tin, pressing the dough well up the sides after trimming. Prick the base of the flan with a fork and allow it to rest in the fridge for 30 minutes.

4 Preheat the oven to 200°C/400°F/Gas 6. Line the flan with greaseproof paper and baking beans. Place the tin on a baking sheet and bake for 20 minutes, removing the paper and beans for the last 5 minutes. When cooked, cool and remove the pastry case from the flan tin.

5 Cream the cheese, lemon curd and lemon rind and juice, adding icing sugar to sweeten, if you wish. Spread the mixture into the base of the flan.

6 Top the flan with the fruits. Gently warm the redcurrant jelly and trickle it over the fruits just before serving the flan decorated with a sprig of mint.

VARIATION

There are all sorts of delightful variations to this recipe. For instance, leave out the redcurrant jelly and sprinkle lightly with icing sugar or decorate with fresh strawberry leaves. Alternatively, top with sliced kiwi fruits or bananas slices sprinkled with lemon juice.

Ginger Baked Pears

This simple French dessert is the kind that would be served after Sunday lunch or a family supper. Try to find Comice or Anjou pears – this recipe is especially useful for slightly under-ripe fruit.

INGREDIENTS

Serves 4

4 large pears

300ml/½ pint/1¼ cups whipping cream

50g/2oz/¼ cup caster sugar

2.5ml/½ tsp vanilla essence

1.5ml/¼ tsp ground cinnamon

pinch of freshly grated nutmeg

5ml/1 tsp grated fresh root ginger

1 Preheat the oven to 190°C/375°F/Gas 5. Lightly butter a large shallow baking dish.

2 Peel the pears, cut in half lengthways and remove the cores. Arrange, cut-side down, in a single layer in the baking dish.

3 Mix together the cream, sugar, vanilla essence, cinnamon, nutmeg and ginger and pour over the pears.

4 Bake for 30–35 minutes, basting from time to time, until the pears are tender and browned on top and the cream is thick and bubbly. Cool slightly before serving.

Prunes Poached in Red Wine

Serve this simple dessert on its own, or with crème fraîche or vanilla ice cream.

INGREDIENTS

Serves 8–10

1 unwaxed orange

1 unwaxed lemon

750ml/1¼ pints/3 cups fruity red wine

50g/2oz/¼ cup caster sugar, or to taste

1 cinnamon stick

pinch of freshly grated nutmeg

2 or 3 cloves

5ml/1 tsp black peppercorns

1 bay leaf

900g/2lb large stoned prunes, soaked in cold water

strips of orange rind, to decorate

cream, to serve

1 Using a vegetable peeler, peel two or three strips of rind from both the orange and lemon. Squeeze the juice from both and put in a large saucepan.

2 Add the wine, sugar, spices, peppercorns, bay leaf, strips of rind to the pan and 475ml/16fl oz/ 2 cups of water.

3 Bring to the boil over a medium heat, stirring occasionally to dissolve the sugar. Drain the prunes and add to the saucepan, reduce the heat to low and simmer, covered, for 10–15 minutes until the prunes are tender. Remove from the heat and set aside until cool.

4 Using a slotted spoon, transfer the prunes to a serving dish. Return the cooking liquid to a medium-high heat and bring to the boil. Boil for 5–10 minutes until slightly reduced and syrupy, then pour or strain over the prunes. Cool, then chill before decorating with strips of orange rind and serving with cream.

Apple Soufflé Omelette

Apples sautéed until they are slightly caramelized make a delicious autumn filling – you could use fresh raspberries or strawberries when they are in seeason.

INGREDIENTS

Serves 2

4 eggs, separated
30ml/2 tbsp single cream
15ml/1 tbsp caster sugar
15g/½oz/1 tbsp butter
icing sugar, for dredging

For the filling
1 eating apple, peeled, cored and sliced
25g/1oz/2 tbsp butter
30ml/2 tbsp soft light brown sugar
45ml/3 tbsp single cream

1 To make the filling, sauté the apple slices in the butter and sugar until just tender. Stir in the cream and keep warm, while making the omelette.

2 Place the egg yolks in a bowl with the cream and sugar and beat well. Whisk the egg whites until they form stiff peaks, then fold into the yolk mixture.

3 Melt the butter in a large heavy-based frying pan, pour in the soufflé mixture and spread evenly. Cook for 1 minute until golden underneath, then cover the pan handle with foil and place under a hot grill to brown the top.

4 Slide the omelette on to a plate, add the apple mixture, then fold over. Sift the icing sugar over thickly, then mark in a criss-cross pattern with a hot metal skewer. Serve immediately.

Blackberry Cobbler

*Make the most of the fresh autumn
blackberries with this juicy dessert.*

INGREDIENTS

Serves 8

800g/1¾lb/6 cups blackberries
200g/7oz/1 cup granulated sugar
20g/¾oz/3 tbsp plain flour
grated rind of 1 lemon
30ml/2 tbsp granulated sugar mixed with
   1.5ml/¼ tsp grated nutmeg

For the topping

225g/8oz/2 cups plain flour
200g/7oz/1 cup granulated sugar
15ml/1 tbsp baking powder
pinch of salt
250ml/8fl oz/1 cup milk
115g/4oz/½ cup butter, melted

1 Preheat the oven to 180°C/
350°F/Gas 4. In a bowl,
combine the blackberries, sugar,
flour and lemon rind. Stir gently to
blend. Transfer to a 2.4 litre/
4 pint/2 quart baking dish.

2 For the topping, sift the flour,
sugar, baking powder and salt
into a large bowl. In a large jug,
combine the milk and butter.

3 Gradually stir the milk
mixture into the dry
ingredients and stir until the batter
is just smooth.

4 Spoon the batter over the
berries, spreading to the edges.

5 Sprinkle the surface with the
sugar and nutmeg mixture.
Bake until the batter topping is set
and lightly browned, about
50 minutes. Serve hot.

COOK'S TIP

If liked, use half blackberries and
half raspberries or tayberries for
the filling.

Greek Fig and Honey Pudding

A quick and easy pudding made from fresh or canned figs topped with thick and creamy Greek-style yogurt, drizzled with honey and sprinkled with pistachio nuts.

INGREDIENTS

Serves 4

4 fresh or canned figs

2 x 225g/8oz tubs/2 cups Greek-style
    strained yogurt

60ml/4 tbsp clear honey

30ml/2 tbsp chopped pistachio nuts

1 Chop the figs and place in the bottom of four stemmed wine glasses or deep, individual dessert bowls.

2 Top each glass or bowl of figs with half a tub (½ cup) of the Greek-style yogurt. Chill until ready to serve.

3 Just before serving drizzle 15ml/1 tbsp of honey over each one and sprinkle with the pistachio nuts.

> ## COOK'S TIP
> ∾
> Try specialist honeys made from clover, acacia or thyme.

Russian Fruit Compote

This fruit pudding is traditionally called "Kissel" and is made from the thickened juice of stewed red or blackcurrants. This recipe uses the whole fruit with an added dash of blackberry liqueur.

INGREDIENTS

Serves 4

225g/8oz/2 cups red or blackcurrants or a
    mixture of both

225g/8oz/1⅓ cups raspberries

50g/2oz/4 tbsp caster sugar

25ml/1½ tbsp arrowroot

15–30ml/1–2 tbsp Crème de Mûre

Greek-style yogurt, to serve

> ## COOK'S TIP
> ∾
> Use Crème de Cassis instead of Crème de Mûre.

1 Place the red or blackcurrants, raspberries and sugar in a pan with 150ml/¼ pint/⅔ cup of water. Cover the pan and cook gently over a low heat for 12–15 minutes, until the fruit is soft.

2 Blend the arrowroot with a little water in a bowl and stir into the fruit. Bring back to the boil, stirring until thickened.

3 Remove from the heat and cool slightly, then gently stir in the Crème de Mûre.

4 Pour into four serving bowls and leave until cold, then chill. Serve topped with spoonfuls of Greek-style yogurt.

Spiced Red Fruit Compote

An aromatic and colourful dessert to serve on a cold day.

Serves 4

4 ripe red plums, halved

225g/8oz/2 cups strawberries, halved

225g/8oz/1⅓ cups raspberries

30ml/2 tbsp light muscovado sugar

1 cinnamon stick

3 pieces star anise

6 cloves

natural yogurt or fromage frais, to serve

1 Place the plums, strawberries and raspberries in a heavy-based pan with the sugar and 30ml/2 tbsp of cold water.

2 Add the cinnamon stick, star anise and cloves to the pan and heat gently, without boiling, until the sugar dissolves and the fruit juices run.

3 Cover the pan and leave the fruit to infuse over a very low heat for about 5 minutes. Remove the spices from the compote before serving warm with natural yogurt or fromage frais.

Rhubarb Spiral Cobbler

Orange in the fruit filling and in the topping gives this pudding added zest.

Serves 4

675g/1½lb rhubarb, sliced

50g/2oz/4 tbsp caster sugar

45ml/3 tbsp orange juice

For the topping

200g/7oz/1⅓ cups self-raising flour

30ml/2 tbsp caster sugar

about 200g/7oz/1 cup natural yogurt

grated rind of 1 medium orange

30ml/2 tbsp demerara sugar

5ml/1 tsp ground ginger

yogurt or custard, to serve

1 Preheat the oven to 200°C/400°F/Gas 6. Cook the rhubarb, sugar and orange juice in a covered pan until tender. Tip into an ovenproof dish.

2 To make the topping, mix the flour and caster sugar, then stir enough of the yogurt to bind to a soft dough.

3 Roll out on a floured surface to a 25cm/10in square. Mix the orange rind, demerara sugar and ginger, then sprinkle this over the surface of the dough.

4 Roll up quite tightly, then cut into about ten slices using a sharp knife. Arrange the slices over the rhubarb.

5 Bake in the oven for 15–20 minutes, or until the spirals are well risen and golden brown. Serve warm, with yogurt or custard.

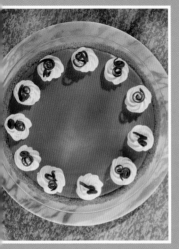

CAKES, PIES
AND TARTS

Chocolate Layer Cake

The cake layers can be made ahead,
wrapped and frozen for future use.
Always defrost cakes completely
before icing.

INGREDIENTS

Serves 10–12

unsweetened cocoa for dusting
225g/8oz can cooked whole beetroot,
    drained and juice reserved
115g/4oz/½ cup unsalted butter, softened
500g/1¼lb/2½ cups light brown sugar,
    firmly packed
3 eggs
15ml/1 tbsp vanilla essence
75g/3oz unsweetened chocolate, melted
275g/10oz/2¼ cups plain flour
10ml/2 tsp baking powder
2.5ml/½ tsp salt
120ml/4fl oz/½ cup buttermilk
chocolate curls (optional)

For the chocolate ganache frosting
475ml/16fl oz/2 cups whipping or
    double cream
500g/1¼lb fine quality, bittersweet or
    semi-sweet chocolate, chopped
15ml/1 tbsp vanilla essence

1 Preheat the oven to 180°C/
350°F/ Gas 4. Grease two
23cm/9in cake tins and dust the
bottom and sides with cocoa.
Grate the beetroot and add to the
juice. With an electric mixer, beat
the butter, brown sugar, eggs and
vanilla until pale and fluffy (for
3–5 minutes). Reduce the speed
and beat in the chocolate.

2 In a bowl, sift the flour, baking
powder and salt. With the
mixer on low speed, alternately
beat in the flour mixture in
quarters and buttermilk in thirds.
Add the beetroot and juice and
beat for 1 minute. Divide between
the tins and bake for 30–35 minutes
or until a cake tester inserted in the
centre comes out clean. Cool for
10 minutes, then unmould and
cool completely.

3 To make the frosting, in a
heavy-based saucepan over
medium heat, heat the cream until
it just begins to boil, stirring
occasionally to prevent scorching.

4 Remove from the heat and stir
in the chocolate, stirring
constantly until melted and
smooth. Stir in the vanilla. Strain
into a bowl and chill, stirring every
10 minutes, until spreadable, for
about 1 hour.

5 Assemble the cake. Place one
layer on a serving plate and
spread with one-third of the
ganache. Turn the cake layer
bottom side up, top with the
second layer, and spread the
remaining ganache over top and
sides of the cake. If using, top with
the chocolate curls. Allow to set for
20–30 minutes, then chill.

Marbled Swiss Roll

Simply sensational – that's the combination of light chocolate sponge and walnut chocolate buttercream.

INGREDIENTS

Serves 6–8

90g/3½oz/scant 1 cup plain flour

15ml/1 tbsp cocoa powder

25g/1oz plain chocolate, grated

25g/1oz white chocolate, grated

3 eggs

115g/4oz/generous ½ cup caster sugar

For the filling

75g/3oz/6 tbsp unsalted butter or
    margarine, softened

175g/6oz/1½ cups icing sugar

15ml/1 tbsp cocoa powder

2.5ml/½ tsp vanilla essence

45ml/3 tbsp chopped walnuts

plain and white chocolate curls, to
    decorate (optional)

1 Preheat the oven to 200°C/ 400°F/Gas 6. Grease a 30 x 20cm/12 x 8in Swiss roll tin and line with non-stick baking paper. Sift half the flour with the cocoa into a bowl. Stir in the grated plain chocolate. Sift the remaining flour into another bowl; stir in the grated white chocolate.

2 Whisk the eggs and sugar in a heatproof bowl; set over a saucepan of hot water until the mixture holds its shape when the whisk is lifted.

3 Remove the bowl from the heat and tip half the mixture into a separate bowl. Fold the white chocolate mixture into one portion, then fold the plain chocolate mixture into the other. Stir 15ml/1 tbsp boiling water into each half to soften the mixtures.

4 Place alternate spoonfuls of mixture in the prepared tin and swirl lightly together for a marbled effect. Bake for about 12–15 minutes, or until firm. Turn out on to a sheet of non-stick baking paper.

5 Trim the edges to neaten and cover with a damp, clean dish towel. Cool.

6 For the filling, beat the butter or margarine, icing sugar, cocoa powder and vanilla essence together in a bowl until smooth, then mix in the walnuts.

7 Uncover the sponge, lift off the baking paper and spread the surface with the buttercream. Roll up carefully from a long side and place on a serving plate. Decorate with plain and white chocolate curls, if wished.

Sponge Cake with Fruit and Cream

Called Génoise, this is the French cake used as the base for both simple and elaborate creations. You could simply dust it with icing sugar, or layer it with seasonal fruits to serve as a seasonal dessert.

INGREDIENTS

Serves 6

115g/4oz/1 cup plain flour

pinch of salt

4 eggs, at room temperature

115g/4oz/scant ⅔ cup caster sugar

2.5ml/½ tsp vanilla essence

50g/2oz/4 tbsp butter, melted or clarified
  and cooled

For the filling

450g/1lb fresh strawberries or raspberries

30–60ml/2–4 tbsp caster sugar

475ml/16fl oz/2 cups whipping cream

5ml/1 tsp vanilla essence

1 Preheat the oven to 180°C/ 350°F/Gas 4. Lightly butter a 23cm/9in springform tin or deep cake tin. Line the base with non-stick baking paper, and dust lightly with flour. Sift the flour and salt together twice.

2 Half-fill a medium saucepan with hot water and set over a low heat (do not allow the water to boil). Put the eggs in a heatproof bowl which just fits into the pan without touching the water. Using an electric mixer, beat the eggs at medium-high speed, gradually adding the sugar, for 8–10 minutes until the mixture is very thick and pale and leaves a ribbon trail when the beaters are lifted. Remove the bowl from the pan, add the vanilla essence and continue beating until the mixture is cool.

3 Fold in the flour mixture in three batches, using a balloon whisk or metal spoon. Before the third addition of flour, stir a large spoonful of the mixture into the melted or clarified butter to lighten it, then fold the butter into the remaining mixture with the last addition of flour. Work quickly, but gently, so the mixture does not deflate. Pour into the prepared tin, smoothing the top so the sides are slightly higher than the centre.

4 Bake in the oven for about 25–30 minutes until the top of the cake springs back when touched and the edge begins to shrink away from the sides of the tin. Place the cake in its tin on a wire rack to cool for 5–10 minutes, then invert the cake on to the rack to cool completely. Peel off the baking paper.

5 To make the filling, slice the strawberries, place in a bowl, sprinkle with 15–30ml/1–2 tbsp of the sugar and set aside. Beat the cream with 15–30ml/1–2 tbsp of the sugar and the vanilla essence until it holds soft peaks.

6 To assemble the cake (up to 4 hours before serving), split the cake horizontally, using a serrated knife. Place the top, cut side up, on a serving plate. Spread with a third of the cream and cover with an even layer of sliced strawberries.

7 Place the bottom half of the cake, cut side down, on top of the filling and press lightly. Spread the remaining cream over the top and sides of the cake. Chill until ready to serve. Serve the remaining strawberries with the cake.

Devil's Food Cake with Orange Frosting

Chocolate and orange are the ultimate combination. Can you resist the temptation?

Serves 8–10

50g/2oz/½ cup unsweetened cocoa powder
175g/6oz/¾ cup butter, at room temperature
350g/12oz/1½ cups dark brown sugar, firmly packed
3 eggs, at room temperature
225g/8oz/2 cups plain flour
25ml/1½ tsp baking soda
1.5ml/¼ tsp baking powder
175ml/6fl oz/¾ cup sour cream
orange rind strips, for decoration

For the frosting
285g/10½oz/1½ cups granulated sugar
2 egg whites
60ml/4 tbsp frozen orange juice concentrate
15ml/1 tbsp fresh lemon juice
grated rind of 1 orange

1 Preheat the oven to 180°C/350°F/Gas 4. Line two 23cm/9in cake tins with greaseproof paper and grease. In a bowl, mix the cocoa and 175ml/6fl oz/¾ cup of boiling water until smooth. Set aside.

2 With an electric mixer, cream the butter and sugar until light and fluffy. Add the eggs, one at a time, beating well.

3 When the cocoa mixture is lukewarm, stir into the butter mixture.

4 Sift together the flour, baking soda and baking powder twice. Fold into the cocoa mixture in three batches, alternating with the sour cream.

5 Pour into the tins. Bake until the cakes pull away from the tin, 30–35 minutes. Stand for 15 minutes before unmoulding.

6 Thinly slice the orange rind strips. Blanch in boiling water for 1 minute.

7 For the frosting, place all the ingredients in the top of a double boiler or in a bowl set over hot water. With an electric mixer, beat until the mixture holds soft peaks. Continue beating off the heat until thick enough to spread.

8 Sandwich the cake with frosting, then spread over the top and sides. Arrange the rind on top.

Black Forest Gâteau

This light chocolate sponge, moistened with Kirsch and layered with cherries and cream, is still one of the most popular of all the chocolate gâteaux.

INGREDIENTS

Serves 8–10

6 eggs

200g/7oz/scant 1 cup caster sugar

5ml/1 tsp vanilla essence

50g/2oz/½ cup plain flour

50g/2oz/½ cup cocoa powder

115g/4oz/½ cup unsalted butter, melted

For the filling and topping

60ml/4 tbsp Kirsch

600ml/1 pint/2½ cups double or whipping
    cream

30ml/2 tbsp icing sugar

2.5ml/½ tsp vanilla essence

675g/1½lb jar stoned morello cherries,
    drained

To decorate

icing sugar, for dusting

grated chocolate

chocolate curls

fresh or drained canned morello cherries

1 Preheat the oven to 180°C/
350°F/Gas 4. Grease three
19cm/7½in sandwich cake tins
and line the base of each with non-
stick baking paper. Whisk the eggs
with the sugar and vanilla essence
in a large bowl until pale and very
thick – the mixture should hold a
firm trail when the whisk is lifted.

2 Sift the flour and cocoa over
the mixture and fold in lightly
and evenly. Stir in the melted
butter. Divide the mixture among
the prepared cake tins, smoothing
them level.

3 Bake for 15–18 minutes, until
risen and springy to the touch.
Leave to cool in the tins for about
5 minutes, then turn out on to wire
racks and leave to cool completely.

4 Prick each layer all over with a
skewer or fork, then sprinkle
with Kirsch. Whip the cream in a
bowl until it starts to thicken, then
beat in the icing sugar and vanilla
essence until the mixture begins to
hold its shape.

5 To assemble, spread one cake
layer with a thick layer of
flavoured cream and top with a
quarter of the cherries. Spread a
second cake layer with cream and
cherries, then place it on top of the
first layer. Top with the final layer.

6 Spread the remaining cream
all over the cake. Dust a plate
with icing sugar; position the cake.
Press grated chocolate over the
sides and decorate with the
chocolate curls and cherries.

Angel Food Cake

This cake is beautifully light. The secret? Sifting the flour over and over again to let plenty of air into it.

INGREDIENTS

Serves 12–14

115g/4oz/1 cup sifted cake flour
285g/10½oz/1½ cups caster sugar
300ml/½ pint/1¼ cups egg whites (about
   10–11 eggs)
6.5ml/1¼ tsp cream of tartar
1.5ml/¼ tsp salt
5ml/1 tsp vanilla essence
1.5ml/¼ tsp almond essence
icing sugar, for dusting

1 Preheat the oven to 160°C/
325°F/Gas 3. Sift the flour
before measuring, then sift it four
times with 90g/3½oz/½ cup of the
sugar. Transfer to a bowl.

2 With an electric mixer, beat
the egg whites until foamy. Sift
over the cream of tartar and salt
and continue to beat until they
hold soft peaks when the beaters
are lifted.

3 Add the remaining sugar in
three batches, beating well
after each addition. Stir in the
vanilla and almond essence.

4 Add the flour mixture, ½ cup
at a time, and fold in gently
with a large metal spoon after
each addition.

5 Transfer to an ungreased
25cm/10in straight-sided ring
mould and bake until delicately
browned on top, about 1 hour.

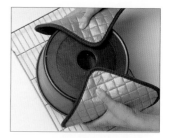

6 Turn the ring mould upside
down on to a cake rack and let
cool for 1 hour. If the cake does
not unmould, run a spatula
around the edge to loosen it. Invert
on to a serving plate.

7 When cool, lay a star-shaped
template on top of the cake,
sift with icing sugar, and lift off.

Chocolate and Cherry Polenta Cake

*Polenta and almonds add an
unusual nutty texture to this
delicious dessert.*

INGREDIENTS

Serves 8

50g/2oz/⅓ cup quick-cook polenta

200g/7oz plain chocolate, broken into
   squares

5 eggs, separated

175g/6oz/¾ cup caster sugar

115g/4oz/1 cup ground almonds

60ml/4 tbsp plain flour

finely grated rind of 1 orange

115g/4oz/½ cup glacé cherries, halved

icing sugar, for dusting

1 Place the polenta in a
heatproof bowl and pour over
just enough boiling water to cover,
about 120ml/4fl oz/½ cup. Stir
well, then cover the bowl and leave
to stand for about 30 minutes,
until the polenta has absorbed all
the excess moisture.

2 Preheat the oven to 190°C/
375°F/Gas 5. Grease a deep
22cm/8½in round cake tin and line
the base with non-stick baking
paper. Melt the chocolate in a
heatproof bowl over hot water.

3 Whisk the egg yolks with the
sugar in a bowl until thick and
pale. Beat in the chocolate, then
fold in the polenta, ground
almonds, flour and orange rind.

4 Whisk the egg whites in a
clean bowl until stiff. Stir
15ml/1 tbsp of the whites into the
chocolate mixture, then fold in the
rest. Finally, fold in the cherries.

5 Scrape the mixture into the
prepared tin and bake for
45–55 minutes or until well risen
and firm to the touch. Cool on a
rack. Dust with icing sugar to serve.

Lemon Coconut Layer Cake

The flavours of lemon and coconut complement each other beautifully in this light dessert cake.

INGREDIENTS

Serves 8–10

175g/6oz/1½ cups plain flour
pinch of salt
7 eggs
350g/12oz/1¾ cups granulated sugar
15ml/1 tbsp grated orange rind
grated rind of 1½ lemons
juice of 1 lemon
65g/2½oz/scant 1 cup desiccated coconut
15ml/1 tbsp cornflour
40g/1½oz/3 tbsp butter

For the frosting

75g/3oz/6 tbsp unsalted butter, at room
    temperature
175g/6oz/1½ cups icing sugar
grated rind of 1½ lemons
30ml/2 tbsp fresh lemon juice
200g/7oz/2½ cups desiccated coconut

1 Preheat the oven to 180°C/
350°F/Gas 4. Line three
20cm/8in cake tins with baking
parchment and grease. In a bowl,
sift together the flour and salt and
set aside.

2 Place six of the eggs in a large
heatproof bowl set over hot
water. With an electric mixer, beat
until frothy. Gradually beat in
225g/8oz/generous 1 cup of the
granulated sugar until the mixture
doubles in volume and is thick
enough to leave a ribbon trail
when the beaters are lifted, which
takes about 10 minutes.

3 Remove the bowl from the hot
water. Fold in the orange rind,
half the grated lemon rind and
15ml/1 tbsp of the lemon juice
until blended. Fold in the coconut.

4 Sift over the flour mixture
in three batches, gently folding
in thoroughly after each addition.

5 Divide the mixture between
the prepared tins.

6 Bake until the cakes pull
away from the sides of the
tin, 20–25 minutes. Leave to stand
for 5 minutes, then turn out and
transfer to a cooling rack.

7 In a bowl, blend the cornflour
with a little cold water to
dissolve. Whisk in the remaining
egg until just blended. Set aside.

8 In a saucepan, combine the
remaining lemon rind and
juice, the remaining sugar, butter
and 120ml/4fl oz/½ cup of water.

9 Over a moderate heat, bring
the mixture to the boil. Whisk
in the eggs and cornflour. Return
to the boil. Whisk constantly until
thick, for about 5 minutes.
Remove from the heat and pour
into a bowl. Cover with baking
parchment and set aside until cool.

10 For the frosting, cream the
butter and icing sugar until
smooth. Stir in the lemon rind and
enough lemon juice to obtain a
thick, spreadable consistency.

11 Sandwich the three cake
layers with the lemon
custard mixture. Spread the
frosting over the top and sides.
Cover the cake with the coconut,
pressing it in gently.

Carrot Cake with Maple Butter Frosting

A good, quick dessert cake for a family supper.

INGREDIENTS

Serves 12

450g/1lb carrots, peeled
175g/6oz/1½ cups plain flour
10ml/2 tsp baking powder
2.5ml/½ tsp baking soda
5ml/1 tsp salt
10ml/2 tsp ground cinnamon
4 eggs
10ml/2 tsp vanilla essence
225g/8oz/1 cup dark brown sugar,
  firmly packed
90g/3½oz/½ cup granulated sugar
300ml/½ pint/1¼ cups sunflower oil
115g/4oz/1 cup walnuts, finely chopped
65g/2½oz/½ cup raisins
walnut halves, for decorating (optional)

For the frosting
75g/3oz/6 tbsp unsalted butter, at room
  temperature
375g/12oz/3 cups icing sugar
50ml/2fl oz/¼ cup maple syrup

1 Preheat the oven to 180°C/
350°F/Gas 4. Line a 28 x 20cm/
11 x 8in rectangular cake tin with
non-stick baking paper and grease.
Grate the carrots and set aside.

2 Sift the flour, baking powder,
baking soda, salt and
cinnamon into a bowl. Set aside.

3 With an electric mixer, beat the
eggs until blended. Add the
vanilla, sugars and oil; beat to
incorporate. Add the dry
ingredients, in three batches,
folding in well after each addition.

4 Add the carrots, walnuts and
raisins and fold in thoroughly.

5 Pour the batter into the
prepared tin and bake until the
cake springs back when touched
lightly, 40–45 minutes. Let stand
10 minutes, then unmould and
transfer to a rack.

6 For the frosting, cream the
butter with half the sugar until
soft. Add the syrup, then beat in
the remaining sugar until blended.

7 Spread the frosting over the
top of the cake. Using a metal
spatula, make decorative ridges.
Cut into squares. Decorate with
walnut halves, if you like.

Black and White Pound Cake

A good cake for packed lunches and picnics as it cuts into neat slices with no messy filling, or serve with custard for dessert.

INGREDIENTS

Serves 16

115g/4oz plain chocolate, broken
   into squares
350g/12oz/3 cups plain flour
5ml/1 tsp baking powder
450g/1lb/2 cups butter, at room
   temperature
650g/1lb 7oz/3⅓ cups sugar
15ml/1 tbsp vanilla essence
10 eggs, at room temperature
icing sugar, for dusting

1 Preheat the oven to 180°C/
350°F/Gas 4. Line the bottom of a 25cm/10in straight-sided ring mould with non-stick baking paper and grease. Dust with flour spread evenly with a brush.

2 Melt the chocolate in the top of a double boiler, or in a heat-proof bowl set over a pan of hot water. Stir occasionally. Set aside.

3 In a bowl, sift together the flour and baking powder. In another bowl, cream the butter, sugar and vanilla essence with an electric mixer until light and fluffy. Add the eggs, two at a time, then gradually incorporate the flour mixture on low speed.

4 Spoon half of the batter into the prepared ring mould.

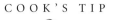

COOK'S TIP

This is also known as Marbled Cake because of its distinctive appearance.

5 Stir the chocolate into the remaining batter, then spoon into the ring mould. With a metal spatula, swirl the two batters to create a marbled effect.

6 Bake until a cake tester inserted in the centre comes out clean, about 1¾ hours. Cover with foil halfway through baking. Let stand 15 minutes, then unmould and transfer to a cooling rack. To serve, dust with icing sugar.

Chocolate Mousse Strawberry Layer Cake

The strawberries used in this cake can be replaced by raspberries or blackberries and the appropriate flavour liqueur.

INGREDIENTS

Serves 10

115g/4oz fine quality white chocolate, chopped

120ml/4fl oz/½ cup whipping or double cream

120ml/4fl oz/½ cup milk

15ml/1 tbsp rum or vanilla essence

115g/4oz/½ cup unsalted butter, softened

175g/6oz/generous ¾ cup granulated sugar

3 eggs

275g/10oz/2½ cups plain flour

5ml/1 tsp baking powder

pinch of salt

675g/1½lb fresh strawberries, sliced, plus extra for decoration

750ml/1¼ pints/3 cups whipping cream

30ml/2 tbsp rum or strawberry-flavoured liqueur

For the white chocolate mousse

250g/9oz fine quality white chocolate, chopped

350ml/12fl oz/1½ cups whipping or double cream

30ml/2 tbsp rum or strawberry-flavoured liqueur

1 Preheat the oven to 180°C/ 350°F/Gas 4. Grease and flour two 23 x 5cm/9 x 2in cake tins. Line the base of the tins with non-stick baking paper. Melt the chocolate and cream in a double boiler over a low heat, stirring until smooth. Stir in the milk and rum or vanilla essence, then set aside to cool.

2 In a large bowl with an electric mixer, beat the butter and sugar until light and creamy. Add the eggs one at a time, beating well.

3 In a small bowl, stir together the flour, baking powder and salt. Alternately add flour and melted chocolate to the eggs in batches, just until blended. Pour the batter evenly into the tins.

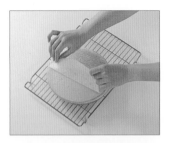

4 Bake for 20–25 minutes until a cake tester inserted in the centre comes out clean. Cool on a wire rack for 10 minutes. Turn the cakes out on to the wire rack, peel off the paper and cool completely.

5 Prepare the mousse. In a medium saucepan over low heat, melt the chocolate and cream until smooth, stirring frequently. Stir in the rum or strawberry-flavoured liqueur and pour into a bowl. Chill until just set. With a wire whisk, whip until the mixture has a "mousse" consistency.

6 Slice both cake layers in half crossways. Sandwich the four layers together with the mousse and strawberries.

7 Whip the cream with the rum or liqueur until firm peaks form. Spread half over the top and sides of the cake. Spoon the remaining cream into an icing bag with a star tip and pipe scrolls on the top. Garnish with the remaining strawberries.

Death by Chocolate

One of the richest chocolate cakes ever, so serve in thin slices.

INGREDIENTS

Serves 16–20

225g/8oz plain dark chocolate, broken
   into squares
115g/4oz/½ cup unsalted butter
150ml/¼ pint/⅔ cup milk
225g/8oz/1¼ cups light muscovado sugar
10ml/2 tsp vanilla essence
2 eggs, separated
150ml/¼ pint/⅔ cup soured cream
225g/8oz/2 cups self-raising flour
5ml/1 tsp baking powder

For the filling

60ml/4 tbsp seedless raspberry jam
60ml/4 tbsp brandy
400g/14oz plain dark chocolate, broken
   into squares
200g/7oz/scant 1 cup unsalted butter

For the topping

250ml/8fl oz/1 cup double cream
225g/8oz plain dark chocolate, broken
   into squares
plain and white chocolate curls,
   to decorate
chocolate-dipped physalis (Cape
   gooseberries), to serve (optional)

1 Preheat the oven to 180°C/350°F/ Gas 4. Grease and base-line a deep 23cm/9in springform cake tin. Place chocolate, butter and milk in a saucepan. Heat gently until smooth. Remove from heat, beat in sugar and vanilla, then cool.

2 Beat the egg yolks and cream in a bowl, then beat into the chocolate mixture. Sift the flour and baking powder over the surface and fold in. Whisk the egg whites in a grease-free bowl until stiff; fold into the mixture.

3 Scrape into the prepared tin and bake for 45–55 minutes, or until firm to the touch. Cool in the tin for 15 minutes, then invert to a wire rack to cool.

4 Slice the cold cake horizontally to make three even layers. In a small saucepan, warm the jam with 15ml/1 tbsp of the brandy, then brush over two of the layers. Heat the remaining brandy in a saucepan with the chocolate and butter, stirring, until smooth. Cool until beginning to thicken.

5 Spread the bottom layer of the cake with half the chocolate filling, taking care not to disturb the jam. Top with a second layer, jam side up, and spread with the remaining filling. Top with the final layer and press lightly. Leave to set.

6 To make the topping, heat the cream and chocolate together in a saucepan over a low heat, stirring frequently until the chocolate has melted. Pour into a bowl, leave to cool, then whisk until the mixture begins to hold its shape.

7 Spread the top and sides of the cake with the chocolate ganache. Decorate with chocolate curls and, if liked, chocolate-dipped physalis (Cape gooseberries).

Simple Chocolate Cake

An easy, everyday chocolate cake which can be filled with butter-cream, or with a rich chocolate ganache for a special occasion.

INGREDIENTS

Serves 6–8

115g/4oz plain chocolate, broken into
squares
45ml/3 tbsp milk
150g/5oz/⅔ cup unsalted butter or
margarine, softened
150g/5oz/scant 1 cup light muscovado
sugar
3 eggs
200g/7oz/1¾ cups self-raising flour
15ml/1 tbsp cocoa powder

For the buttercream
75g/3oz/6 tbsp unsalted butter or
margarine, softened
175g/6oz/1½ cups icing sugar
15ml/1 tbsp cocoa powder
2.5ml/½ tsp vanilla essence
icing sugar and cocoa powder, for dusting

1 Preheat the oven to 180°C/
350°F/Gas 4. Grease two
18cm/7in round sandwich cake
tins and line the base of each with
non-stick baking paper. Melt the
chocolate with the milk in a
heatproof bowl set over a pan of
simmering water.

2 Cream the butter or
margarine with the sugar in a
mixing bowl until pale and fluffy.
Add the eggs one at a time, beating
well after each addition. Stir in the
chocolate mixture until it is
well combined.

3 Sift the flour and cocoa over
the mixture and fold in with
a metal spoon until evenly mixed.
Scrape into the prepared tins,
smooth level and bake for
35–40 minutes or until well risen
and firm. Turn out on wire racks
and leave to cool.

4 To make the buttercream, beat
the butter or margarine, icing
sugar, cocoa powder and vanilla
essence together in a bowl until the
mixture is smooth.

5 Sandwich the cake layers
together with the buttercream.
Dust with a mixture of icing sugar
and cocoa just before serving.

Pineapple Upside-Down Cake

This is a perennial favourite to serve in winter or summer.

INGREDIENTS

Serves 8

115g/4oz/½ cup butter

225g/8oz/1 cup dark brown sugar, firmly packed

450g/16oz can pineapple slices, drained

4 eggs, separated

grated rind of 1 lemon

pinch of salt

90g/3½oz/½ cup granulated sugar

85g/3¼oz/¾ cup plain flour

5ml/1 tsp baking powder

1 Preheat the oven to 180°C/ 350°F/Gas 4. Melt the butter in an ovenproof cast-iron frying pan, about 25cm/10in in diameter. Remove 15ml/1 tbsp of the melted butter and set aside.

2 Add the brown sugar to the frying pan and stir until blended. Place the drained pineapple slices on top in one layer. Set aside.

3 In a bowl, whisk together the egg yolks, reserved butter and lemon rind until smooth and well blended. Set aside.

4 With an electric mixer, beat the egg whites with the salt until stiff. Fold in the granulated sugar, 30ml/2 tbsp at a time. Fold in the egg yolk mixture.

5 Sift the flour and baking powder together. Fold into the egg mixture in three batches.

6 Pour the batter over the pineapple and smooth level.

7 Bake until a cake tester inserted in the centre comes out clean, about 30 minutes.

8 While still hot, place a serving plate on top of the frying pan, bottom-side up. Holding them together with oven gloves, flip over. Serve hot or cold.

Peach and Blueberry Pie

The unusual combination of fruits in this pie looks especially good with a lattice pastry topping.

INGREDIENTS

Serves 8

225g/8oz/2 cups plain flour
pinch of salt
10ml/2 tsp sugar
150g/5oz/10 tbsp cold butter or margarine
1 egg yolk
30ml/2 tbsp milk, to glaze

For the filling

450g/1lb fresh peaches, peeled, stoned
   and sliced
275g/10oz/2 cups fresh blueberries
150g/5oz/¾ cup caster sugar
30ml/2 tbsp fresh lemon juice
40g/1½oz/⅓ cup plain flour
large pinch of grated nutmeg
25g/1oz/2 tbsp butter or margarine, cut
   into tiny pieces

1 To make the pastry, sift the flour, salt and sugar into a bowl. Rub the butter or margarine into the dry ingredients as quickly as possible until the mixture resembles coarse breadcrumbs.

2 Mix the egg yolk with 50ml/ 2fl oz/¼ cup of iced water and sprinkle over the flour mixture. Combine with a fork until the dough holds together. If the dough is too crumbly, add a little more water, 15ml/1 tbsp at a time. Gather the dough into a ball and flatten into a round. Place in a sealed polythene bag and chill for at least 20 minutes.

3 Roll out two-thirds of the pastry between two sheets of greaseproof paper to a thickness of about 3mm/⅛in. Use to line a 23cm/9in pie dish.

4 Trim the pastry all around, leaving a 1cm/½in overhang. Fold the overhang under to form the edge. Using a fork, press the edge to the rim of the pie dish.

5 Gather the trimmings and remaining pastry into a ball, and roll out to a thickness of about 5mm/¼in. Using a pastry wheel or sharp knife, cut into long, 1cm/½in wide strips. Chill both the pastry case and the strips of pastry for 20 minutes. Meanwhile, preheat the oven to 200°C/400°F/Gas 6.

6 Line the pastry case with greaseproof paper and fill with dried beans. Bake for 7–10 minutes, until the pastry is just set. Remove from the oven and carefully lift out the paper with the beans. Prick the base of the pastry case with a fork, then return to the oven and bake for a further 5 minutes. Leave to cool slightly before filling. Leave the oven on.

7 For the filling, place the peach slices and blueberries in a bowl and stir in the sugar, lemon juice, flour and nutmeg. Spoon the fruit mixture into the pastry case. Dot the top with the pieces of butter or margarine.

8 Weave a lattice top with the chilled pastry strips, pressing the ends to the edge of the baked pastry case. Brush the strips with the milk.

9 Bake the pie for 15 minutes. Reduce the oven temperature to 180°C/350°F/Gas 4, and continue baking for another 30 minutes, until the filling is tender and bubbling and the pastry lattice is golden. If the pastry becomes too brown, cover loosely with a piece of foil. Serve the pie warm or at room temperature.

COOK'S TIP

Don't over-chill the pastry strips. If they become too firm, they may crack and break as you weave them into a lattice.

Rhubarb Pie

Use a biscuit cutter to cut out decorative pastry shapes and make this pie extra special.

INGREDIENTS

Serves 6

175g/6oz/1½ cups plain flour
2.5ml/½ tsp salt
10ml/2 tsp caster sugar
75g/3oz/6 tbsp cold butter or margarine
30ml/2 tbsp single cream
single or double cream, to serve

For the filling
1kg/2¼lb fresh rhubarb, cut into
  2.5cm/1in slices
30ml/2 tbsp cornflour
1 egg
275g/10oz/1½ cups caster sugar
15ml/1 tbsp grated orange rind

1 To make the pastry, sift the flour, salt and sugar into a bowl. Using a pastry blender or two knives, cut the butter or margarine into the dry ingredients as quickly as possible until the mixture resembles breadcrumbs.

2 Sprinkle the flour mixture with about 50ml/2fl oz/¼ cup of iced water and mix until the dough just holds together. If the dough is too crumbly, add a little more water, 15ml/1 tbsp at a time.

3 Gather the dough into a ball, flatten into a round, place in a polythene bag and put in the fridge for 20 minutes.

4 Roll out the pastry between two sheets of greaseproof paper to a 3mm/⅛in thickness. Use to line a 23cm/9in pie dish or tin. Trim all around, leaving a 1cm/½in overhang. Fold the overhang under the edge and flute. Chill the case and trimmings for 30 minutes.

5 To make the filling, put the rhubarb in a bowl, sprinkle with the cornflour and toss to coat.

6 Preheat the oven to 220°C/ 425°F/Gas 7. Beat the egg with the sugar in a bowl until thoroughly blended, then mix in the orange rind.

7 Stir the sugar mixture into the rhubarb and mix well together, then spoon the fruit into the prepared pastry case.

8 Roll out the pastry trimmings. Stamp out decorative shapes with a biscuit cutter.

9 Arrange the pastry shapes on top of the pie. Brush the shapes and the edge of the pastry case with cream.

10 Bake the pie for 30 minutes. Reduce the oven temperature to 160°C/325°F/Gas 3 and continue baking for a further 15–20 minutes, until the pastry is golden brown and the rhubarb is tender. Serve the pie hot with cream.

Chocolate Pecan Torte

This torte uses finely ground nuts instead of flour. Toast then cool the nuts before grinding finely in a blender or food processor. Do not over-grind the nuts, as the oils will form a paste.

INGREDIENTS

Serves 16

200g/7oz bittersweet or plain chocolate, chopped

150g/5oz/10 tbsp unsalted butter, cut into pieces

4 eggs

90g/3½oz/½ cup caster sugar

10ml/2 tsp vanilla essence

115g/4oz/1 cup ground pecans

10ml/2 tsp ground cinnamon

24 toasted pecan halves to decorate (optional)

For the chocolate honey glaze

115g/4oz bittersweet or semi-sweet chocolate, chopped

60g/2oz/¼ cup unsalted butter, cut into pieces

30ml/2 tbsp clear honey

pinch of ground cinnamon

1 Preheat oven to 180°C/350°F/ Gas 4. Grease a 20 x 5cm/8 x 2in springform tin; line with baking paper then grease the paper. Wrap the bottom and sides of the tin with foil to prevent water seeping in. In a saucepan over a low heat, melt the chocolate and butter, stirring until smooth. Remove from the heat. In a mixing bowl with the electric mixer, beat the eggs, sugar and vanilla essence until frothy, 1–2 minutes. Stir in the melted chocolate, ground nuts and cinnamon. Pour into the prepared tin.

2 Place the foil-wrapped tin in a large roasting tin and pour boiling water into the roasting tin, to come 2cm/¾in up the side of the springform tin. Bake for 25–30 minutes until the edge of the cake is set, but the centre is soft. Remove the tin from the water bath and remove the foil. Cool on a rack.

3 Prepare the glaze. In a small saucepan over low heat, melt the chocolate, butter, honey and cinnamon, stirring until smooth; remove from the heat. Carefully dip the toasted pecan halves halfway into the glaze and place on a non-stick baking-paper-lined baking sheet until it is set.

4 Remove the sides from the tin and invert the cake on to a wire rack. Remove the tin bottom and paper, so the bottom of the cake is now the top. Pour the thickened glaze over the cake, tilting the rack slightly to spread the glaze. Use a metal palette knife to smooth the sides. Arrange the glazed nuts around outside edge of the torte and allow the glaze to set.

Key Lime Pie

Key limes come from Florida but if they are not available, ordinary limes will do just as well.

INGREDIENTS

Serves 8

3 large egg yolks
400g/14oz can sweetened condensed milk
15ml/1 tbsp grated Key lime rind
120ml/4fl oz/½ cup fresh Key lime juice
green food colouring (optional)
120ml/4fl oz/½ cup whipping cream

For the crust
1¼ cups digestive biscuit crumbs
75ml/5 tbsp butter or margarine, melted

1 Preheat the oven to 180°C/350°F/Gas 4. For the crust, place the biscuit crumbs in a bowl and add the butter or margarine. Mix to combine.

2 Press the crumbs evenly over the bottom and sides of a 23cm/9in pie dish or tin. Bake for 8 minutes. Let cool.

3 Beat the yolks until thick. Beat in the milk, lime rind and juice, and colouring, if using. Pour into the prebaked pie crust and refrigerate until set, about 4 hours. To serve, whip the cream. Pipe a lattice pattern on top, or spoon dollops around the edge.

Fruit Tartlets

The chocolate pastry cases make a dramatic base to these tartlets.

INGREDIENTS

Makes 8

215g/7½oz/¾ cup redcurrant or grape jelly
15ml/1 tbsp fresh lemon juice
175ml/6fl oz/¾ cup whipping cream
675g/1½lb fresh fruit, such as strawberries, raspberries, kiwi fruit, peaches, grapes or blueberries, peeled and sliced as necessary

For the pastry
150g/5oz/⅔ cup cold butter, cut in pieces
65g/2½oz/⅓ cup dark brown sugar, firmly packed
45ml/3 tbsp unsweetened cocoa powder
175g/6oz/1½ cups plain flour
1 egg white

1 For the pastry, combine the butter, brown sugar and cocoa over low heat. When the butter is melted, remove from the heat and sift over the flour. Stir, then add just enough egg white to bind the mixture. Gather into a ball, wrap in greaseproof paper, and chill for at least 30 minutes.

2 Preheat the oven to 180°C/350°F/Gas 4. Grease eight 7.5cm/3in tartlet tins. Roll out the dough between two sheets of greaseproof paper and stamp out eight 10cm/4in rounds with a fluted cutter.

3 Line the tartlet tins with dough. Prick the bottoms. Chill for 15 minutes.

4 Bake until firm, 20–25 minutes. Leave to cool, then remove from the tins.

5 Melt the jelly with the lemon juice. Brush a thin layer in the bottom of the tartlets. Whip the cream and spread a thin layer in the tartlet shells. Arrange the fruit on top. Brush evenly with the glaze and serve.

Cherry Pie

The woven lattice is the perfect finishing touch, although you can cheat and use a lattice pastry roller if you prefer.

INGREDIENTS

Serves 8

900g/2lb fresh Morello cherries, stoned, or
  2 x 450g /1lb cans or jars, drained and
  stoned
65g/2½oz/generous ¾ cup caster sugar
25g/1oz/¼ cup plain flour
25ml/1½ tbsp fresh lemon juice
1.5ml/¼ tsp almond essence
25g/1oz/2 tbsp butter or margarine

For the pastry
225g/8oz/2 cups plain flour
5ml/1 tsp salt
175g/6oz/¾ cup lard or vegetable fat

1 For the pastry, sift the flour and salt into a mixing bowl. Using a pastry blender, cut in the fat until the mixture resembles coarse breadcrumbs.

2 Sprinkle in 60–75ml/4–5 tbsp iced water, a tablespoon at a time, tossing lightly with your fingertips or a fork until the pastry forms a ball.

3 Preheat the oven to 220°C/ 425°F/Gas 7. Divide the pastry in half and shape each half into a ball. On a lightly floured surface, roll out one of the balls to a circle about 30cm/12in in diameter.

4 Use it to line a 23cm/9in pie tin, easing the pastry in and being careful not to stretch it. With scissors, trim off excess pastry, leaving a 1cm/½in overhang around the pie tin.

5 Roll out the remaining pastry to 3mm/⅛in thick. Cut out eleven strips 1cm/½in wide.

6 In a mixing bowl, combine the cherries, sugar, flour, lemon juice and almond essence. Spoon the mixture into the pastry case and dot the top with the butter or margarine.

7 To make the lattice, place five of the pastry strips evenly across the filling. Fold every other strip back. Lay the first strip across in the opposite direction. Continue in this pattern, folding back every other strip each time you add a cross strip.

8 Trim the ends of the lattice strips even with the case overhang. Press together so that the edge rests on the pie-tin rim. With your thumbs, flute the edge. Chill for 15 minutes.

9 Bake the pie for 30 minutes, covering the edge of the pastry case with foil, if necessary, to prevent over-browning. Let cool, in the tin, on a wire rack.

Mince Pies with Orange Cinnamon Pastry

Home-made mince pies are so much nicer than shop bought, especially with this tasty pastry.

INGREDIENTS

Makes 18

225g/8oz/2 cups plain flour
40g/1½oz icing sugar
10ml/2 tsp ground cinnamon
150g/5oz/10 tbsp butter
grated rind of 1 orange
225g/8oz/⅔ cup mincemeat
1 beaten egg, to glaze
icing sugar, to dust

1 Sift together the flour, icing sugar and cinnamon then rub in the butter until it forms crumbs. (This can be done in a food processor.) Stir in the grated orange rind.

2 Mix to a firm dough with about 60ml/4 tbsp ice cold water. Knead lightly, then roll out to a 5mm/¼in thickness.

3 Using a 6cm/2½in round cutter, cut out 18 circles, re-rolling as necessary. Then cut out 18 smaller 5cm/2in circles.

4 Line two bun tins with the 18 larger circles – they will fill one and a half tins. Spoon a small spoonful of mincemeat into each pastry case and top with the smaller pastry circles, pressing the edges lightly together to seal.

5 Glaze the tops of the pies with egg and leave to rest in the fridge for 30 minutes. Preheat the oven to 200°C/400°F/Gas 6.

6 Bake the pies for 15–20 minutes until they are golden brown. Remove them to wire racks to cool. Serve just warm and dusted with icing sugar.

Apple-Cranberry Lattice Pie

Use fresh or frozen cranberries for this classic American pie.

INGREDIENTS

Serves 8

grated rind of 1 orange
45ml/3 tbsp fresh orange juice
2 large, tart cooking apples
115g/4oz/1 cup cranberries
65g/2½oz/½ cup raisins
25g/1oz/¼ cup walnuts, chopped
225g/8oz/1 cup granulated sugar
115g/4oz/½ cup dark brown sugar
15ml/1 tbsp quick-cooking tapioca

For the pastry
225g/8oz/2 cups plain flour
2.5ml/½ tsp salt
90ml/6 tbsp cold butter, cut in pieces
60ml/4 tbsp cold lard, cut in pieces
15ml/1 tbsp granulated sugar,
    for sprinkling

1 For the pastry, sift the flour and salt into a bowl. Add the butter and lard and rub in until the mixture resembles coarse crumbs. With a fork, stir in just enough iced water to bind the dough. Gather into two equal balls, wrap in greaseproof paper, and chill for at least 20 minutes.

2 Put the orange rind and juice into a mixing bowl. Peel and core the apples and grate them into the bowl. Stir in the cranberries, raisins, walnuts, granulated sugar, brown sugar and tapioca.

3 Place a baking sheet in the oven and preheat to 200°C/400°F/Gas 6.

4 On a lightly floured surface, roll out one ball of dough about 3mm/⅛in thick. Transfer to a 23cm/9in pie tin and trim the edge. Spoon the cranberry and apple mixture into the shell.

5 Roll out the remaining dough to a circle about 28cm/11in in diameter. With a serrated pastry wheel, cut the dough into ten strips, 2cm/¾in wide. Place five strips horizontally across the top of the tart at 1-inch intervals. Weave in six vertical strips. Trim the edges. Sprinkle the top with 15ml/1 tbsp of sugar.

6 Bake for 20 minutes. Reduce the heat to 180°C/350°F/Gas 4 and bake until the crust is golden and the filling is bubbling, about 15 minutes more.

Lemon Meringue Pie

Serve this exactly as it is, hot, warm or cold. It doesn't need any accompaniment.

INGREDIENTS

Serves 8

grated rind and juice of 1 large lemon

200g/7oz/1 cup caster sugar

25g/1oz/2 tbsp butter

45ml/3 tbsp cornflour

3 eggs, separated

pinch of salt

0.75ml/⅛ tsp cream of tartar

For the pastry

115g/4oz/1 cup plain flour

2.5ml/½ tsp salt

65g/2½oz/⅓ cup cold lard, cut in pieces

1 For the pastry, sift the flour and salt into a bowl. Add the lard and cut in with a pastry blender until the mixture resembles coarse crumbs. With a fork, stir in just enough iced water to bind the dough (about 30ml/ 2 tbsp). Gather the dough into a ball.

2 On a lightly floured surface, roll out the dough to 3mm/⅛in thick. Transfer to a 23cm/9in pie tin and trim the edge to leave a 1cm/½in overhang.

3 Fold the overhang under and crimp the edge. Chill the pie shell in the fridge for at least 20 minutes. Preheat the oven to 200°C/400°F/Gas 6.

4 Prick the dough all over with a fork. Line with greaseproof paper and fill with baking beans. Bake for 12 minutes. Remove the paper and beans and continue baking until golden, about 6–8 minutes more.

5 In a saucepan, combine the lemon rind and juice, 90g/ 3½oz/½ cup of the sugar, butter and 250ml/8fl oz/1 cup of water. Bring the mixture to the boil.

6 Meanwhile, in a mixing bowl, dissolve the cornflour in 15ml/1 tbsp of cold water. Add the egg yolks.

7 Add the egg yolks to the lemon mixture and return to the boil, whisking continuously until the mixture thickens, about 5 minutes.

8 Cover the surface with grease-proof paper to prevent a skin forming and let cool.

9 For the meringue, using an electric mixer beat the egg whites with the salt and cream of tartar until they hold stiff peaks. Add the remaining sugar and beat until glossy.

10 Spoon the lemon mixture into the pie shell and spread level. Spoon the meringue on top, smoothing it up to the edge of the crust to seal. Bake until golden, 12–15 minutes.

Chocolate Chiffon Pie

This light and creamy dessert is as luxurious as its name suggests.

INGREDIENTS

Serves 8

175g/6oz plain chocolate squares

25g/1oz square bitter chocolate

250ml/8fl oz/1 cup milk

15ml/1 tbsp gelatine, or alternative

130g/4½oz/⅔ cup granulated sugar

2 size 1 eggs, separated

5ml/1 tsp vanilla essence

350ml/12fl oz/1½ cups whipping cream

pinch of salt

whipped cream and chocolate curls, to
   decorate

For the crust

75g/3oz/1½ cups digestive biscuit crumbs

75g/3oz/6 tbsp butter, melted

1 Place a baking sheet in the oven and preheat to 180°C/ 350°F/Gas 4. For the crust, mix the digestive biscuit crumbs and butter in a bowl. Press the crumbs evenly over the bottom and sides of a 23cm/9in pie tin. Bake for 8 minutes. Let cool.

2 Chop the chocolate, then grind in a food processor or blender. Set aside.

3 Place the milk in the top of a double boiler or in a heatproof bowl. Sprinkle over the gelatine. Let stand 5 minutes to soften.

4 Set the top of the double boiler or heatproof bowl over hot water. Add 50g/2oz/⅓ cup of the sugar, the chocolate and egg yolks. Stir until dissolved. Add the vanilla essence.

5 Set the top of the double boiler in a bowl of ice and stir until the mixture reaches room temperature. Remove from the ice and set aside.

6 Whip the cream lightly. Set aside. With an electric mixer, beat the egg whites and salt until they hold soft peaks. Add the remaining sugar and beat only enough to blend.

7 Fold a dollop of egg whites into the chocolate mixture, then pour back into the whites and gently fold in.

8 Fold in the whipped cream and pour into the pastry shell. Put in the freezer until just set, about 5 minutes. If the centre sinks, fill with any remaining mixture. Chill for 3–4 hours. Decorate with whipped cream and chocolate curls. Serve cold.

Coconut Cream Pie

Once you have made the pastry, the delicious filling can be put together in moments.

INGREDIENTS

Serves 8

200g/7oz/2½ cups shredded coconut

115g/4oz/⅔ cup caster sugar

60ml/4 tbsp cornflour

pinch of salt

600ml/1 pint/2½ cups milk

50ml/2fl oz/¼ cup whipping cream

2 egg yolks

25g/1oz/2 tbsp unsalted butter

10ml/2 tsp vanilla essence

For the pastry

115g/4oz/1 cup plain flour

1.5ml/¼ tsp salt

40g/1½oz/3 tbsp cold butter, cut in pieces

25g/1oz/2 tbsp cold lard

1 For the pastry, sift the flour and salt into a bowl. Add the butter and lard and cut in with a pastry blender or two knives until the mixture resembles coarse breadcrumbs.

2 With a fork, stir in just enough iced water to bind the dough (30–45ml/2–3 tbsp). Gather into a ball, wrap in greaseproof paper and chill for at least 20 minutes.

3 Preheat the oven to 220°C/ 425°F/Gas 7. Roll out the dough 3mm/⅛in thick. Transfer to a 23cm/9in flan tin. Trim and flute the edges. Prick the bottom. Line with greaseproof paper and fill with baking beans. Bake for 10–12 minutes. Remove the paper and beans, reduce the heat to 180°C/350°F/Gas 4 and bake until brown, about 10–15 minutes more.

4 Spread 75g/3oz/1 cup of the coconut on a baking sheet and toast in the oven until golden, 6–8 minutes, stirring often. Set aside for decorating.

5 Put the sugar, cornflour and salt in a saucepan. In a bowl, whisk together the milk, cream and egg yolks. Add the egg mixture to the saucepan.

6 Cook over low heat, stirring constantly, until the mixture comes to the boil. Boil for 1 minute, then remove from the heat. Add the butter, vanilla essence and remaining coconut.

7 Pour into the pre-baked pastry case. When the filling is cool, sprinkle toasted coconut in a ring in the centre.

Peach Tart with Almond Cream

The almond cream filling should be baked until it is just turning brown. Take care not to overbake it or the delicate flavours will be spoilt.

Serves 8–10

4 large ripe peaches
115g/4oz/⅔ cup blanched almonds
30ml/2 tbsp plain flour
90g/3½oz/7 tbsp unsalted butter, at room
   temperature
130g/4½oz/scant ¾ cup granulated sugar
1 egg
1 egg yolk
2.5ml/½ tsp vanilla essence, or 10ml/
   2 tsp rum

For the pastry
150g/5oz/1¼ cups flour
4ml/¾ tsp salt
90g/3½oz/7 tbsp cold unsalted butter, cut
   in pieces
1 egg yolk

1 For the pastry, sift the flour and salt into a bowl.

2 Add the butter and cut in with a pastry blender until the mixture resembles coarse crumbs. With a fork, stir in the egg yolk and just enough iced water (30–45ml/ 2–3 tbsp) to bind the dough. Gather into a ball, wrap in grease-proof paper and chill for at least 20 minutes. Place a baking sheet in the oven and preheat to 200°C/400°F/Gas 6.

3 On a lightly floured surface, roll out the pastry 3mm/⅛in thick. Transfer to a 25cm/10in flan tin. Trim the edge, prick the bottom and chill.

4 Score the bottoms of the peaches. Drop the peaches, one at a time, into boiling water. Leave for 20 seconds, then dip in cold water. Peel off the skins using a sharp knife.

5 Grind the almonds finely with the flour in a food processor, blender or nut grinder. With an electric mixer, cream the butter and 90g/3½oz/½ cup of the sugar until light and fluffy. Gradually beat in the egg and yolk. Stir in the almonds and vanilla or rum. Spread in the pastry shell.

6 Halve the peaches and remove the stones. Cut crosswise in thin slices and arrange on top of the almond cream like the spokes of a wheel; keep the slices of each peach-half together. Fan them out by pressing down gently at a slight angle.

7 Bake until the pastry begins to brown, 10–15 minutes. Lower the heat to 180°C/350°F/Gas 4 and continue baking until the almond cream sets, about 15 minutes more. Ten minutes before the end of the cooking time, sprinkle with the remaining sugar.

VARIATION

For a Nectarine and Apricot Tart with Almond Cream, replace the peaches with nectarines, prepared and arranged the same way. Peel and chop three fresh apricots. Fill the spaces between the fanned-out nectarines with chopped apricots. Bake as above.

Raspberry Tart

This glazed fruit tart really does taste as good as it looks.

Serves 8

4 egg yolks

65g/2½ oz/⅓ cup granulated sugar

45ml/3 tbsp plain flour

300ml/½ pint/1¼ cups milk

pinch of salt

2.5ml/½ tsp vanilla essence

450g/1lb fresh raspberries

75ml/5 tbsp grape or redcurrant jelly

15ml/1 tbsp fresh orange juice

For the pastry

150g/5oz/1¼ cups plain flour

2.5ml/½ tsp baking powder

1.5ml/¼ tsp salt

15ml/1 tbsp sugar

grated rind of ½ orange

90ml/6 tbsp cold butter, cut in pieces

1 egg yolk

45–60ml/3–4 tbsp whipping cream

1 For the pastry, sift the flour, baking powder and salt into a bowl. Stir in the sugar and orange rind. Add the butter and mix until the mixture resembles coarse crumbs. With a fork, stir in the egg yolk and just enough cream to bind the dough. Gather into a ball, wrap in greaseproof paper and chill.

2 For the custard filling, beat the egg yolks and sugar until thick and lemon-coloured. Gradually stir in the flour.

3 In a saucepan, bring the milk and salt just to the boil, and remove from the heat. Whisk into the egg yolk mixture, return to the pan, and continue whisking over moderately high heat until just bubbling. Cook for 3 minutes to thicken. Transfer immediately to a bowl. Stir in the vanilla to blend.

4 Cover with greaseproof paper to prevent a skin from forming.

5 Preheat the oven to 200°C/400°F/Gas 6. On a lightly floured surface, roll out the dough about 3mm/⅛in thick, transfer to a 25cm/10in flan tin and trim the edge. Prick the bottom all over with a fork and line with greaseproof paper. Fill with baking beans and bake for 15 minutes. Remove the paper and baking beans. Continue baking until golden, 6–8 minutes more. Let cool.

6 Spread an even layer of the pastry cream filling in the tart shell and arrange the raspberries on top. Melt the jelly and orange juice in a pan over a low heat and brush on top to glaze.

Kiwi Ricotta Cheese Tart

*It is well worth taking your time
arranging the kiwi fruit topping in
neat rows for this exotic and
impressive-looking tart.*

INGREDIENTS

Serves 8

50g/2oz/½ cup blanched almonds

90g/3½oz/½ cup plus 15ml/1 tbsp
   caster sugar

900g/2lb/4 cups ricotta cheese

250ml/8fl oz/1 cup whipping cream

1 egg

3 egg yolks

15ml/1 tbsp plain flour

pinch of salt

30ml/2 tbsp rum

grated rind of 1 lemon

40ml/2½ tbsp lemon juice

50ml/2fl oz/¼ cup clear honey

5 kiwi fruit

For the pastry

150g/5oz/1¼ cups plain flour

15ml/1 tbsp granulated sugar

2.5ml/½ tsp salt

2.5ml/½ tsp baking powder

75g/3oz/6 tbsp cold butter, cut in pieces

1 egg yolk

45–60ml/3–4 tbsp whipping cream

1 For the pastry, sift the flour, sugar, salt and baking powder into a bowl. Cut in the butter until the mixture resembles coarse crumbs. Mix the egg yolk and cream. Stir in just enough to bind the dough.

2 Transfer to a lightly floured surface, flatten slightly, wrap in greaseproof paper and chill for 30 minutes. Preheat the oven to 220°C/425°F/Gas 7.

3 On a lightly floured surface, roll out the dough 3mm/⅛in thick and transfer to a 23cm/9in springform tin. Crimp the edge.

4 Prick the bottom of the dough all over with a fork. Line with greaseproof paper and fill with baking beans. Bake for 10 minutes. Remove the paper and beans and bake until golden, 6–8 minutes more. Let cool. Reduce the heat to 180°C/350°F/Gas 4.

5 Grind the almonds finely with 15ml/1 tbsp of the sugar in a food processor or blender.

6 With an electric mixer, beat the ricotta until creamy. Add the cream, egg, yolks, remaining sugar, flour, salt, rum, lemon rind and 30ml/2 tbsp of the lemon juice. Beat to combine.

7 Stir in the ground almonds until well blended.

8 Pour into the shell and bake until golden, about 1 hour. Let cool, then chill, loosely covered, for 2–3 hours. Unmould and place on a serving plate.

9 Combine the honey and remaining lemon juice for the glaze. Set aside.

10 Peel the kiwis. Halve them lengthwise, then cut crosswise into 5mm/¼in slices. Arrange the slices in rows across the top of the tart. Just before serving, brush with the glaze.

Lemon and Orange Tart

Refreshing citrus fruits in a crisp, nutty pastry case.

INGREDIENTS

Serves 8–10

115g/4oz/1 cup plain flour, sifted
115g/4oz/1 cup wholemeal flour
25g/1oz/3 tbsp ground hazelnuts
25g/1oz/3 tbsp icing sugar, sifted
pinch of salt
115g/4oz/½ cup unsalted butter
60ml/4 tbsp lemon curd
300ml/½ pint/1¼ cups whipped cream or fromage frais
4 oranges, peeled and thinly sliced

1 Place the flours, hazelnuts, sugar, salt and butter in a food processor and process in short bursts until the mixture resembles breadcrumbs. Add 30–45ml/2–3 tbsp cold water and process until the dough comes together.

2 Turn out on to a lightly floured surface and knead gently until smooth. Roll out and line a 25cm/10in flan tin. Ease the pastry gently into the corners without stretching it. Chill for 20 minutes. Preheat the oven to 190°C/375°F/Gas 5.

3 Line the pastry with grease-proof paper and fill with baking beans. Bake blind for 15 minutes, remove the paper and beans and continue for a further 5–10 minutes, until the pastry is crisp. Allow to cool.

4 Whisk the lemon curd into the cream or fromage frais and spread over the base of the pastry. Arrange the orange slices on top and serve at room temperature.

Chocolate Pear Tart

Serve slices of this drizzled with single cream or with a scoop of vanilla ice cream for a special treat.

Serves 8

115g/4oz plain chocolate, grated

3 large firm, ripe pears

1 egg

1 egg yolk

120ml/4fl oz/½ cup single cream

2.5ml/½ tsp vanilla essence

45ml/3 tbsp caster sugar

For the pastry

115g/4oz/1 cup plain flour

pinch of salt

30ml/2 tbsp caster sugar

115g/4oz/½ cup cold unsalted butter, cut into pieces

1 egg yolk

15ml/1 tbsp fresh lemon juice

1 For the pastry, sift the flour and salt into a bowl. Add the sugar and butter. Cut in with a pastry blender until the mixture resembles coarse crumbs. With a fork, stir in the egg yolk and lemon juice until the mixture forms a dough. Gather into a ball, wrap in greaseproof paper, and chill for at least 20 minutes.

2 Place a baking sheet in the oven and preheat to 200°C/400°F/Gas 6. On a lightly floured surface, roll out the dough to 3mm/⅛in thick and trim the edge. Transfer to a 25cm/10in flan tin.

3 Sprinkle the bottom of the tart shell with the grated chocolate.

4 Peel, halve and core the pears. Cut in thin slices crosswise, then fan them out slightly.

5 Transfer the pear halves to the tart with the help of a metal spatula and arrange on top of the chocolate to resemble the spokes of a wheel.

6 Whisk together the egg and egg yolk, cream and vanilla essence. Ladle over the pears, then sprinkle with sugar.

7 Bake for 10 minutes. Reduce the heat to 180°C/350°F/Gas 4 and cook until the custard is set and the pears begin to caramelize, about 20 minutes more. Serve at room temperature.

Blueberry-Hazelnut Cheesecake

The base for this cheesecake is made with ground hazelnuts – a tasty and unusual alternative to a biscuit base.

INGREDIENTS

Serves 6–8

350g/12oz blueberries
15ml/1 tbsp clear honey
75g/3oz/6 tbsp granulated sugar
juice of 1 lemon
175g/6oz/¾ cup cream cheese, at room
    temperature
1 egg
5ml/1 tsp hazelnut liqueur (optional)
120ml/4fl oz/½ cup whipping cream

For the base

175g/6oz/1⅔ cups ground hazelnuts
75g/3oz/⅔ cup plain flour
pinch of salt
50g/2oz/4 tbsp butter, at room
    temperature
65g/2½oz/⅓ cup light brown sugar,
    firmly packed
1 egg yolk

1 For the base, put the hazelnuts in a large bowl. Sift in the flour and salt, and stir to mix. Set aside.

2 Beat the butter with the brown sugar until light and fluffy. Beat in the egg yolk. Gradually fold in the nut mixture, in three batches, until well combined.

3 Press the dough into a greased 23cm/9in pie tin, spreading it evenly against the sides. Form a rim around the top edge that is slightly thicker than the sides. Cover and chill for at least 30 minutes.

4 Preheat the oven to 180°C/350°F/Gas 4. Meanwhile, for the topping, combine the blueberries, honey, 15ml/1 tbsp of the granulated sugar and 5ml/1 tsp lemon juice in a heavy saucepan. Cook the mixture over low heat, stirring occasionally, until the berries have given off some liquid but still retain their shape, 5–7 minutes. Remove from the heat and set aside.

5 Place the pastry base in the oven and bake for 15 minutes. Remove and let cool while making the filling.

6 Beat together the cream cheese and remaining granulated sugar until light and fluffy. Add the egg, 15ml/1 tbsp lemon juice, the liqueur, if using, and the cream and beat until thoroughly blended.

7 Pour the cheese mixture into the pastry base and spread evenly. Bake until just set, 20–25 minutes.

8 Let the cheesecake cool completely on a wire rack, then cover and chill for at least 1 hour.

9 Spread the blueberry mixture evenly over the top of the cheesecake. Serve at cool room temperature.

COOK'S TIP
~
The cheesecake can be prepared 1 day in advance, but add the fruit shortly before serving.

Raspberry and White Chocolate Cheesecake

Raspberries and white chocolate are an irresistible combination, especially when teamed with rich mascarpone on a crunchy ginger and pecan nut base.

INGREDIENTS

Serves 8

50g/2oz/4 tbsp unsalted butter
225g/8oz/2⅓ cups ginger nut biscuits, crushed
50g/2oz/½ cup chopped pecan nuts or walnuts

For the filling

275g/10oz/1¼ cups mascarpone cheese
175g/6oz/¾ cup fromage frais
2 eggs, beaten
45ml/3 tbsp caster sugar
250g/9oz white chocolate, broken into squares
225g/8oz/1⅓ cups fresh or frozen raspberries

For the topping

115g/4oz/½ cup mascarpone cheese
75g/3oz/⅓ cup fromage frais
white chocolate curls and raspberries, to decorate

2 Make the filling. Beat the mascarpone and fromage frais in a bowl, then beat in the eggs and caster sugar until evenly mixed.

3 Melt the white chocolate gently in a heatproof bowl over hot water.

4 Stir the chocolate into the cheese mixture with the raspberries.

5 Tip into the prepared tin and spread evenly, then bake for about 1 hour or until just set. Switch off the oven, but do not remove the cheesecake. Leave it until cold and completely set.

6 Release the tin and lift the cheesecake on to a plate. Make the topping by mixing the mascarpone and fromage frais in a bowl and spread over the cheesecake. Decorate with chocolate curls and raspberries.

1 Preheat the oven to 150°C/300°F/Gas 2. Melt the butter in a saucepan, then stir in the crushed biscuits and nuts. Press into the base of a 23cm/9in spring-form cake tin.

Treacle Tart

Quite a filling tart, this, so best served after a light main course.

INGREDIENTS

Serves 4–6

175ml/6fl oz/¾ cup golden syrup
75g/3oz/1½ cups fresh white bread-
    crumbs
grated rind of 1 lemon
30ml/2 tbsp fresh lemon juice

For the pastry

150g/5oz/1¼ cups flour
2.5ml/½ tsp salt
75g/3oz/6 tbsp cold butter, cut in pieces
75g/3oz/3 tbsp cold margarine, cut
    in pieces

1 For the pastry, combine the flour and salt in a bowl. Add the butter and margarine and cut in with a pastry blender until the mixture resembles coarse crumbs.

2 With a fork, stir in just enough iced water (about 45–60ml/ 3–4 tbsp) to bind the dough. Gather into a ball, wrap in grease-proof paper, and chill for at least 20 minutes.

3 On a lightly floured surface, roll out the dough 3mm/⅛in thick. Transfer to a 20cm/8in flan tin and trim off the overhang. Chill for at least 20 minutes. Reserve the trimmings for the lattice top.

4 Place a baking sheet above the centre of the oven and heat to 200°C/400°F/Gas 6.

5 In a saucepan, warm the syrup until thin and runny.

6 Remove from the heat and stir in the breadcrumbs and lemon rind. Let sit for 10 minutes so the bread can absorb the syrup. Add more breadcrumbs if the mixture is thin. Stir in the lemon juice and spread evenly in the pastry shell.

7 Roll out the pastry trimmings and cut into 10–12 thin strips.

8 Lay half the strips on the filling, then carefully arrange the remaining strips to form a lattice pattern.

9 Place on the hot sheet and bake for 10 minutes. Lower the heat to 190°C/375°F/Gas 5. Bake until golden, about 15 minutes more. Serve warm or cold.

Rich Chocolate-Berry Tart

Use any berries you like to top this exotic tart.

Serves 10

115g/4oz/½ cup unsalted butter, softened

90g/3½oz/⅓ cup caster sugar

2.5ml/½ tsp salt

15ml/1 tbsp vanilla essence

50g/2oz/½ cup unsweetened cocoa

215g/7½oz/1¾ cups plain flour

450g/1lb fresh berries for topping

For the chocolate ganache filling

475ml/16fl oz/2 cups double cream

150g/5oz/½ cup seedless blackberry preserve

225g/8oz plain chocolate, chopped

25g/1oz/2 tbsp unsalted butter

For the blackberry sauce

225g/8oz fresh or frozen blackberries or raspberries

15ml/1 tbsp lemon juice

25g/1oz/2 tbsp caster sugar

30ml/2 tbsp blackberry liqueur

1 Prepare the pastry. Place the butter, sugar, salt and vanilla in a food processor and process until creamy. Add the cocoa and process for 1 minute. Add the flour all at once and process for 10–15 seconds, until just blended. Place a piece of clear film on a work surface. Turn out the dough on to the clear film. Use the film to help shape the dough into a flat disc and wrap tightly. Chill for 1 hour.

2 Lightly grease a 23cm/9in tart tin with a removable base. Roll out the dough between two sheets of clear film to a 28cm/11in round, about 5 mm/¼in thick. Peel off the top sheet of clear film, invert the dough and ease it into the tin. Remove the clear film.

3 With floured fingers, press the dough on to the base and sides of the tin, then roll a rolling pin over the edge of the tin to cut off any excess dough. Prick the base with a fork. Chill for 1 hour. Preheat the oven to 180°C/350°F/Gas 4. Line tart shell with foil or baking paper; fill with baking beans. Bake for 10 minutes; lift out the foil with the beans and bake for 5 minutes more, until just set (the pastry may look underdone on the bottom, but it will dry out). Remove to a wire rack to cool.

4 Prepare the filling. In a medium saucepan over medium heat, bring the cream and blackberry preserve to the boil. Remove from the heat and add the chocolate, stirring until smooth. Stir in the butter and strain into the cooled tart, smoothing the top. Cool the tart completely.

5 Prepare the sauce. In a food processor combine the blackberries, lemon juice and sugar, and process until smooth. Strain into a bowl and add the liqueur. If it is too thick, thin with a little water.

6 To serve, remove the tart from the tin. Place on a serving plate and arrange the berries on top. With a pastry brush, brush with a little of the blackberry sauce to glaze lightly. Serve the remaining sauce separately.

Bakewell Tart

*Although the pastry base makes this
a tart, the original recipe describes it
as a pudding.*

INGREDIENTS

Serves 4

225g/8oz ready-made puff pastry

30ml/2 tbsp raspberry or apricot jam

2 eggs

2 egg yolks

115g/4oz/generous ½ cup caster sugar

115g/4oz/½ cup butter, melted

50g/2oz/½ cup ground almonds

few drops of almond essence

icing sugar, for sifting

1 Preheat the oven to 200°C/
400°F/Gas 6. Roll out the
pastry on a lightly floured surface
and use it to line an 18cm/7in pie
plate or loose-based flan tin.
Spread the jam over the bottom of
the pastry case.

COOK'S TIP

Since this pastry case isn't baked
blind first, place a baking sheet
in the oven while it preheats,
then place the flan tin on the hot
sheet. This will ensure that the
bottom of the pastry case cooks
right through.

2 Whisk the eggs, egg yolks and
sugar together in a large bowl
until thick and pale.

3 Gently stir the butter, ground
almonds and almond essence
into the mixture.

4 Pour the mixture into the
pastry case and bake for
30 minutes, until the filling is just
set and browned. Sift icing sugar
over the top before serving the tart
hot, warm or cold.

VARIATION

Ground hazelnuts are increasingly
available and make an interesting
change to the almonds in this tart.
If you are going to grind shelled
hazelnuts yourself, first roast them
in the oven for 10–15 minutes to
bring out their flavour then rub in
a dish towel to remove skins.

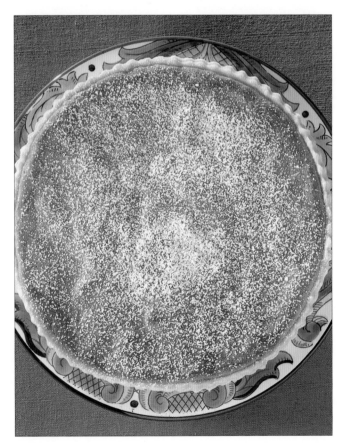

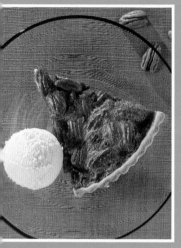

INTERNATIONAL CLASSICS

~

Apple Pie

Delicious on its own, or with a dollop of double cream or ice cream.

INGREDIENTS

Serves 8

900g/2lb tart cooking apples
30ml/2 tbsp plain flour
90g/3½oz/½ cup sugar
25ml/1½ tbsp fresh lemon juice
2.5ml/½ tsp ground cinnamon
2.5ml/½ tsp ground allspice
1.5ml/¼ tsp ground ginger
1.5ml/¼ tsp grated nutmeg
1.5ml/¼ tsp salt
50g/2oz/4 tbsp butter, diced

For the pastry

225g/8oz/2 cups plain flour
5ml/1 tsp salt
75g/3oz/6 tbsp cold butter, cut in pieces
50g/2oz/4 tbsp cold lard, cut in pieces

1 For the pastry, sift the flour and salt into a bowl.

2 Add the butter and lard and cut in with a pastry blender or rub between your fingertips until the mixture resembles coarse crumbs. With a fork, stir in just enough iced water to bind the dough (60–120ml/4–8 tbsp).

3 Gather into two balls, wrap in greaseproof paper and chill for 20 minutes.

4 On a lightly floured surface, roll out one dough ball to 3mm/⅛in thick. Transfer to a 23cm/9in pie tin and trim the edge. Place a baking sheet in the centre of the oven and preheat to 220°C/425°F/Gas 7.

5 Peel, core and slice the apples into a bowl. Toss with the flour, sugar, lemon juice, spices and salt. Spoon into the pie shell; dot with butter.

6 Roll out the remaining dough. Place on top of the pie and trim to leave a 2cm/¾in overhang. Fold the overhang under the bottom dough and press to seal. Crimp the edge.

7 Roll out the scraps and cut out leaf shapes and roll balls for the holly decoration. Arrange on top of the pie. Cut steam vents.

8 Bake for 10 minutes. Reduce the heat to 180°C/350°F/Gas 4 and bake until golden, 40–45 minutes more. If the pie browns too quickly, protect with foil.

Apple Brown Betty

This simple dessert tastes good with cream or ice cream.

INGREDIENTS

Serves 6

50g/2oz/1 cup fresh breadcrumbs
50g/2oz/¾ cup light brown sugar,
  firmly packed
2.5ml/½ tsp ground cinnamon
1.5ml/¼ tsp ground cloves
1.5ml/¼ tsp grated nutmeg
50g/2oz/4 tbsp butter
900g/2lb tart-sweet apples
juice of 1 lemon
50g/2oz/⅓ cup finely chopped walnuts

1 Preheat the grill. Spread the breadcrumbs on a baking sheet and toast under the grill until golden, stirring so they colour evenly. Set aside.

2 Preheat the oven to 190°C/375°F/Gas 5. Butter a 2.4 litre/4 pint/2 quart baking dish. Set aside.

3 Mix the sugar with the spices. Cut the butter into pea-size pieces. Set aside.

4 Peel, core and slice the apples. Toss immediately with the lemon juice to prevent the apple slices from turning brown.

5 Sprinkle about 40ml/2½ tbsp of breadcrumbs over the bottom of the prepared dish. Cover with a third of the apple slices and sprinkle with a third of the sugar-spice mixture. Add another layer of breadcrumbs and dot with a third of the butter. Repeat the layers two more times, ending with a layer of bread-crumbs. Sprinkle with the nuts, and dot with the remaining butter.

6 Bake until the apples are tender and the top is golden brown, 35–40 minutes. Serve warm or cold.

American Spiced Pumpkin Pie

The unofficial national dish of the United States.

INGREDIENTS

Serves 4–6

175g/6oz/1½ cups plain flour

pinch of salt

75g/3oz/6 tbsp unsalted butter

15ml/1 tbsp caster sugar

450g/1lb/4 cups peeled fresh pumpkin, cubed, or 400g/14oz/2 cups canned pumpkin, drained

115g/4oz/½ cup soft light brown sugar

1.5ml/¼ tsp salt

1.5ml/¼ ground allspice

2.5ml/½ tsp ground cinnamon

2.5ml/½ tsp ground ginger

2 eggs, lightly beaten

120ml/4fl oz/½ cup double cream

whipped cream, to serve

1 Place the flour in a bowl with the salt and butter and rub with your fingertips until the mixture resembles breadcrumbs (or use a food processor).

2 Stir in the sugar and add about 30-45ml/2-3 tbsp water and mix to a soft dough. Knead the dough lightly on a floured surface. Flatten out into a round, wrap in a polythene bag and chill for 1 hour.

3 Preheat the oven to 200°C/400°F/Gas 6 with a baking sheet inside. If you are using raw pumpkin for the pie, steam for 15 minutes until quite tender, then leave to cool completely. Purée the steamed or canned pumpkin in a food processor or blender until it is very smooth.

4 Roll out the pastry quite thinly and use to line a 24cm/9½in (measured across the top) x 2.5cm/1in deep pie tin. Trim off any excess pastry and reserve for the decoration. Prick the base of the pastry case with a fork.

5 Cut as many leaf shapes as you can from the excess pastry and make vein markings with the back of a knife on each. Brush the edge of the pastry with water and stick the leaves all round the edge. Chill.

6 In a large bowl mix together the pumpkin purée, sugar, salt, spices, eggs and cream and pour into the prepared pastry case. Smooth the top with a knife.

7 Place on the preheated baking sheet and bake for 15 minutes. Then reduce the temperature to 180°C/350°F/Gas 4 and cook for a further 30 minutes, or until the filling is set and the pastry golden. Serve the pie warm with a generous dollop of whipped cream.

Classic Cheesecake

You can decorate this with fruit and serve it with cream, if you like, but it tastes delicious just as it is.

INGREDIENTS

Serves 8

25g/1oz/½ cup digestive biscuit crumbs
900g/2lb cream cheese
250g/9oz/1¼ cups caster sugar
grated rind of 1 lemon
45ml/3 tbsp fresh lemon juice
5ml/1 tsp vanilla essence
4 eggs, at room temperature

1 Preheat the oven to 160°C/ 325°F/Gas 3. Grease a 23cm/8in springform cake tin. Place on a round of foil 13cm/5in larger than the diameter of the pan. Press it up the sides to seal tightly.

2 Sprinkle the crumbs in the base of the pan. Press to form an even layer.

3 With an electric mixer, beat the cream cheese until smooth. Add the sugar, lemon rind and juice and vanilla essence, and beat until blended. Beat in the eggs, one at a time. Beat just enough to blend thoroughly.

4 Pour into the prepared tin. Set the tin in a larger baking tray and place in the oven. Pour enough hot water in the outer tray to come 2.5cm/1in up the side of the tin.

5 Bake until the top of the cake is golden brown, about 1½ hours. Let cool in the tin.

6 Run a knife around the edge to loosen, then remove the rim of the tin. Chill for at least 4 hours before serving.

Chocolate Cheesecake

This popular variation of the classic dessert is made with a cinnamon and chocolate base.

INGREDIENTS

Serves 10–12

175g/6oz plain chocolate squares
115g/4oz bitter chocolate squares
1.15kg/2½lb cream cheese, at room
    temperature
200g/7oz/1 cup caster sugar
10ml/2 tsp vanilla essence
4 eggs, at room temperature
175ml/6fl oz/¾ cup sour cream

For the base

75g/3oz/1½ cups chocolate wafer crumbs
75g/3oz/6 tbsp butter, melted
2.5ml/½ tsp ground cinnamon

1 Preheat the oven to 180°C/350°F/Gas 4. Grease a 23cm/9in springform cake tin.

2 For the base, mix the chocolate wafer crumbs with the butter and cinnamon. Press evenly in the bottom of the tin.

3 Melt the plain and bitter chocolate in the top of a double boiler, or in a heatproof bowl set over hot water. Set aside.

4 With an electric mixer, beat the cream cheese until smooth, then beat in the sugar and vanilla essence. Add the eggs, one at a time, scraping the bowl with a spatula when necessary.

5 Add the sour cream. Stir in the melted chocolate.

6 Pour into the tin and bake for 1 hour. Allow to cool in the tin. Remove the rim and chill before serving.

Mississippi Pecan Pie

This fabulous dessert started life in the United States but has become an international favourite.

INGREDIENTS

Serves 6–8

For the pastry

115g/4oz/1 cup plain flour
50g/2oz/4 tbsp butter, cubed
25g/1oz/2 tbsp caster sugar
1 egg yolk

For the filling

175g/6oz/½ cup golden syrup
50g/2oz/⅓ cup dark muscovado sugar
50g/2oz/4 tbsp butter
3 eggs, lightly beaten
2.5ml/½ tsp vanilla essence
150g/5oz/1¼ cups pecan nuts
fresh cream or ice cream, to serve

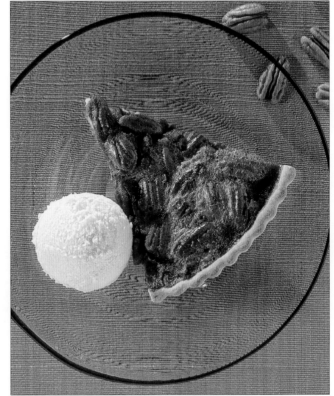

1 Place the flour in a bowl and add the butter. Rub in the butter with your fingertips until the mixture resembles bread-crumbs, then stir in the sugar, egg yolk and about 30ml/2 tbsp cold water. Mix to a dough and knead lightly on a floured surface until smooth.

2 Roll out the pastry and use to line a 20cm/8in loose-based fluted flan tin. Prick the base, then line with greaseproof paper and fill with baking beans. Chill for 30 minutes. Preheat the oven to 200°C/400°F/Gas 6.

3 Bake the pastry case for 10 minutes. Remove the paper and beans and bake for 5 minutes. Reduce the oven temperature to 180°C/350°F/Gas 4.

4 Meanwhile, heat the syrup, sugar and butter in a pan until the sugar dissolves. Remove from the heat and cool slightly. Whisk in the eggs and vanilla essence and stir in the pceans.

5 Pour into the pastry case and bake for 35–40 minutes, until the filling is set. Serve with cream or ice cream.

Boston Banoffee Pie

*There are many variations of this
American treat; this one is easy to
make and tastes wonderful.*

INGREDIENTS

Serves 6–8

150g/5oz/1¼ cups plain flour
225g/8oz/1 cup butter
50g/2oz/4 tbsp caster sugar
½ x 405g/14oz can skimmed, sweetened
    condensed milk
115g/4oz/⅔ cup soft light brown sugar
30ml/2 tbsp golden syrup
2 small bananas, sliced
a little lemon juice
whipped cream, to decorate
5ml/1 tsp grated plain chocolate

1 Preheat the oven to 160°C/
325°F/Gas 3. Place the flour
and 115g/4oz/½ cup of the butter
in a food processor and blend
until crumbed (or rub in with
your fingertips). Stir in the
caster sugar.

2 Squeeze the mixture together
until it forms a dough. Press
into the base of a 20cm/8in loose-
based fluted flan tin. Bake for
25–30 minutes.

3 Place the remaining butter
with the condensed milk,
brown sugar and golden syrup in a
large non-stick saucepan and heat
gently, stirring, until the butter has
melted and the sugar has dissolved.

4 Bring to a gentle boil and cook
for 7 minutes, stirring all the
time (to prevent burning), until
the mixture thickens and turns a
light caramel colour. Pour on to
the cooked pastry base and leave
until cold.

5 Sprinkle the bananas with
lemon juice and arrange in
overlapping circles on top of the
caramel filling, leaving a gap in the
centre. Pipe a swirl of whipped
cream in the centre and sprinkle
with the grated chocolate.

Vermont Baked Maple Custard

Try to find pure maple syrup for this custard as it will really enhance the flavour.

INGREDIENTS

Serves 6

3 eggs

120ml/4fl oz/½ cup maple syrup

600ml/1 pint/2½ cups milk

pinch of salt

pinch of grated nutmeg

1 Preheat the oven to 180°C/350°F/Gas 4. Combine all the ingredients in a large bowl and mix together thoroughly.

2 Set individual custard cups or ramekins in a roasting tin half filled with hot water. Pour the custard mixture into the cups. Bake until the custards are set, 45 minutes–1 hour. Test by inserting the blade of a knife in the centre: it should come out clean. Serve warm or chilled.

Crème Caramel

Crème caramel, or crème renversée, is one of the most popular French desserts and is wonderful when freshly made. This is a slightly lighter modern version of the traditional recipe.

INGREDIENTS

Serves 6–8

250g/9oz/1¼ cups granulated sugar

60ml/4 tbsp water

1 vanilla pod or 10ml/2 tsp vanilla essence

400ml/14fl oz/1⅔ cups milk

250ml/8fl oz/1 cup whipping cream

5 large eggs

2 egg yolks

1 Put 175g/6oz/⅞ cup of the sugar in a small heavy saucepan with 60ml/4 tbsp of water to moisten. Bring to the boil over a high heat, swirling the pan to dissolve the sugar. Boil, without stirring, until the syrup turns a dark caramel colour (this will take about 4–5 minutes).

2 Immediately pour the caramel into a 1 litre/1¾ pint/4 cup soufflé dish. Holding the dish with oven gloves, quickly swirl the dish to coat the base and sides with the caramel and set aside. (The caramel will harden quickly as it cools.) Place the dish in a small roasting tin.

3 Preheat the oven to 160°C/325°F/Gas 3. With a small sharp knife, carefully split the vanilla pod lengthways and scrape the black seeds into a medium saucepan, or add the vanilla essence. Add the milk and cream and bring just to the boil over a medium-high heat, stirring frequently. Remove the pan from the heat, cover and set aside for 15–20 minutes.

4 In a bowl, whisk the eggs and egg yolks with the remaining sugar for 2–3 minutes until smooth and creamy. Whisk in the hot milk and carefully strain the mixture into the caramel-lined dish. Cover with foil.

5 Place the dish in a roasting tin and pour in enough boiling water to come halfway up the sides of the dish. Bake the custard for 40–45 minutes until just set and a knife inserted about 5cm/2in from the edge comes out clean. Remove from the roasting tin and cool for at least 30 minutes, then chill overnight.

6 To turn out, carefully run a sharp knife around the edge of the dish to loosen the custard. Cover the dish with a serving plate and, holding them tightly, invert the dish and plate together. Gently lift one edge of the dish, allowing the caramel to run over the sides, then slowly lift off the dish.

Apple Strudel

This Austrian pudding is tradition-
ally made with paper-thin layers of
buttered strudel pastry, filled with
spiced apples and nuts. Ready-made
filo pastry makes an easy substitute.

INGREDIENTS

Serves 4–6

75g/3oz/¾ cup hazelnuts, chopped
    and roasted
30ml/2 tbsp nibbed almonds, roasted
50g/2oz/4 tbsp demerara sugar
2.5ml/½ tsp ground cinnamon
grated rind and juice of ½ lemon
2 large Bramley cooking apples, peeled,
    cored and chopped
50g/2oz/⅓ cup sultanas
4 large sheet filo pastry
50g/2oz/4 tbsp unsalted butter, melted
icing sugar, for dusting

1 Preheat the oven to 190°C/
375°F/Gas 5. In a bowl mix
together the hazelnuts, almonds,
sugar, cinnamon, lemon rind
and juice, apples and sultanas.
Set aside.

2 Lay one sheet of filo pastry on
a clean dish towel and brush
with melted butter. Lay a second
sheet on top and brush again with
melted butter. Repeat with the
remaining two sheets.

3 Spread the fruit and nut
mixture over the pastry,
leaving a 7.5cm/3in border at the
shorter ends. Fold the ends in
over the filling. Roll up from one
long edge, using the dish towel.

4 Transfer the strudel to a
greased baking sheet, placing
it seam side down. Brush with
butter and bake for 30–35 minutes,
until golden and crisp. Dust with
icing sugar and serve hot with
cream, custard or yogurt.

Chocolate Fruit Fondue

Fondues originated in Switzerland
and this sweet treat is the perfect
ending to any meal.

INGREDIENTS

Serves 6–8

16 fresh strawberries
4 rings fresh pineapple, cut into wedges
2 small nectarines, stoned and cut
    into wedges
1 kiwi fruit, halved and thickly sliced
small bunch of black seedless grapes
2 bananas, chopped
1 small eating apple, cored and cut
    into wedges
lemon juice, for brushing
225g/8oz plain chocolate
15g/½oz/1 tbsp butter
150ml/¼ pint/⅔ cup single cream
45ml/3 tbsp Irish cream liqueur
15ml/1 tbsp pistachio nuts, chopped

1 Arrange the fruit on a serving
platter and brush the banana
and apple pieces with a little lemon
juice. Cover and place in the fridge
until ready to serve.

2 Place the chocolate, butter,
cream and liqueur in a
bowl over a pan of simmering
water. Stir until melted and
completely smooth.

3 Pour the mixture into a
warmed serving bowl; sprinkle
with pistachios. Guests help
themselves by skewering fruits on to
forks and dipping in the hot sauce.

Floating Islands

Originally these oval-shaped meringues were poached in milk and this was then used to make the rich custard sauce.

INGREDIENTS

Serves 4–6

1 vanilla pod
600ml/1 pint/2½ cups milk
8 egg yolks
50g/2oz/¼ cup granulated sugar

For the meringues
4 size 1 egg whites
1.5ml/¼ tsp cream of tartar
225g/8oz/1¼ cups caster sugar

For the caramel
150g/5oz/¾ cup granulated sugar

1 Split the vanilla pod lengthways and scrape the seeds into a saucepan. Add the milk and bring just to the boil over a medium heat, stirring frequently. Cover and set aside for 15–20 minutes.

2 In a medium bowl, whisk the egg yolks and sugar for 2–3 minutes until thick and creamy. Whisk in the hot milk and return the mixture to the saucepan. With a wooden spoon, stir over a medium-low heat until the sauce begins to thicken and coat the back of the spoon (do not allow to boil). Immediately strain into a chilled bowl, allow to cool, stirring occasionally and then chill.

3 Half-fill a large wide frying pan or saucepan with water and bring just to simmering point. In a clean, grease-free bowl, whisk the egg whites until frothy. Add the cream of tartar and continue whisking until they form soft peaks. Sprinkle over the caster sugar, about 30ml/2 tbsp at a time, and whisk until the whites are stiff and glossy.

4 Using two tablespoons, form egg-shaped meringues and slide them into the water (you may need to work in batches). Poach them for 2–3 minutes, turning once until just firm. Using a large slotted spoon, transfer the cooked meringues to a baking sheet lined with kitchen paper to drain.

5 Pour the cold custard into individual serving dishes and arrange the meringues on top.

6 To make the caramel, put the sugar into a small saucepan with 45ml/3 tbsp of water to moisten. Bring to the boil over a high heat, swirling the pan to dissolve the sugar. Boil, without stirring, until the syrup turns a dark caramel colour. Immediately drizzle the caramel over the meringues and custard in a zig-zag pattern. Serve cold. (The caramel will soften if made too far ahead.)

Crème Brûlée

This dessert actually originated in Cambridge, but has become associated with France and is widely eaten there. Add a little liqueur, if you like, but it is equally delicious without it.

INGREDIENTS

Serves 6

1 vanilla pod
1 litre/1¾ pints/4 cups double cream
6 egg yolks
90g/3½oz/½ cup caster sugar
30ml/2 tbsp almond or orange liqueur
    (optional)
75g/3oz/⅓ cup soft light brown sugar

1 Preheat the oven to 150°C/300°F/Gas 2. Place six 120ml/4fl oz/½ cup ramekins in a roasting tin and set aside.

2 With a small sharp knife, split the vanilla pod lengthways and scrape the black seeds into a medium saucepan. Add the cream and bring just to the boil over a medium heat, stirring. Remove from the heat and cover. Set aside for 15–20 minutes.

3 In a bowl, whisk the egg yolks, caster sugar and liqueur, if using, until well blended. Whisk in the hot cream and strain into a large jug. Divide the custard equally among the ramekins.

4 Pour enough boiling water into the roasting tin to come halfway up the sides of the ramekins. Cover the tin with foil and bake for about 30 minutes until the custards are just set. Remove from the tin and leave to cool. Return to the dry roasting tin and chill.

5 Preheat the grill. Sprinkle the sugar evenly over the surface of each custard and grill for 30–60 seconds until the sugar melts and caramelizes. (Do not let the sugar burn or the custard curdle.) Place in the fridge to set the crust and chill completely before serving.

COOK'S TIP

To test if the custards are ready, push the point of a knife into centre of one – if it comes out clean, the custards are cooked.

Crêpes Suzette

This is one of the best-known French desserts and is easy to do at home. You can make the crêpes in advance, then you will be able to put the dish together quickly at the last minute.

INGREDIENTS

Serves 6

115g/4oz/1 cup plain flour

1.5ml/¼ tsp salt

25g/1oz/2 tbsp caster sugar

2 eggs, lightly beaten

250ml/8fl oz/1 cup milk

30ml/2 tbsp orange flower water or
    orange liqueur (optional)

25g/1oz/2 tbsp unsalted butter, melted,
    plus more for frying

For the orange sauce

75g/3oz/6 tbsp unsalted butter

50g/2oz/¼ cup caster sugar

grated rind and juice of 1 large
    unwaxed orange

grated rind and juice of 1 unwaxed lemon

150ml/¼ pint/⅔ cup fresh orange juice

60ml/4 tbsp orange liqueur, plus more for
    flaming (optional)

brandy, for flaming (optional)

orange segments, to decorate

1 In a medium bowl, sift together the flour, salt and sugar. Make a well in the centre and pour in the beaten eggs. Using an electric whisk, beat the eggs, bringing in a little flour until it is all incorporated. Slowly whisk in the milk and 60ml/4 tbsp water to make a smooth batter.

2 Whisk in the orange flower water or liqueur, if using, then strain the batter into a large jug and set aside for 20–30 minutes. If the batter thickens, add a little milk or water to thin.

3 Heat an 18–20cm/7–8in crêpe pan over a medium heat. Stir the melted butter into the crêpe batter. Brush the hot pan with a little extra melted butter and pour in about 30ml/2 tbsp of batter. Quickly tilt and rotate the pan to cover the base with a thin layer of batter. Cook for about 1 minute until the top is set and the base is golden. With a palette knife, carefully turn over the crêpe and cook for 20–30 seconds, just to set. Tip out on to a plate.

4 Continue cooking the crêpes, stirring the batter occasionally and brushing the pan with a little melted butter as and when necessary. Place a sheet of clear film between each crêpe as they are stacked to prevent sticking.

5 To make the sauce, melt the butter in a large frying pan over a medium-low heat, then stir in the sugar, orange and lemon rind and juice, the additional orange juice and the orange liqueur, if using.

6 Place a crêpe in the pan golden side down, swirling gently to coat with the sauce. Fold it in half, then in half again to form a triangle and push to the side of the pan. Continue heating and folding the crêpes until all are warm and covered with the sauce.

7 To flame the crêpes, heat 30–45ml/2–3 tbsp each of orange liqueur and brandy in a small saucepan over a medium heat. Remove the pan from the heat, carefully ignite the liquid with a match then gently pour over the crêpes. Scatter over the orange segments and serve at once.

Tarte au Citron

You can find this classic lemon tart in bistros all over France.

INGREDIENTS

Serves 8–10

350g/12oz shortcrust or sweet shortcrust
    pastry
grated rind of 2 or 3 lemons
150ml/¼ pint/⅔ cup freshly squeezed
    lemon juice
90g/3½oz/½ cup caster sugar
60ml/4 tbsp crème fraîche or double
    cream
4 eggs, plus 3 egg yolks
icing sugar, for dusting

1 Preheat the oven to 190°C/ 375°F/Gas 5. Roll out the pastry thinly and use to line a 23cm/9in flan tin. Prick the base of the pastry.

2 Line the pastry case with foil and fill with baking beans. Bake for about 15 minutes until the edges are set and dry. Remove the foil and beans and continue baking for a further 5–7 minutes until golden.

3 Place the lemon rind, juice and sugar in a bowl. Beat until combined and then gradually add the crème fraîche or double cream and beat until well blended.

4 Beat in the eggs, one at a time, then beat in the egg yolks and pour the filling into the pastry case. Bake for 15–20 minutes, until the filling is set. If the pastry begins to brown too much, cover the edges with foil. Leave to cool. Dust with a little icing sugar before serving.

Pear and Almond Cream Tart

This tart is equally successful made with other kinds of fruit, and some variation can be seen in almost every good French pâtisserie. Try making it with nectarines, peaches, apricots or apples.

INGREDIENTS

Serves 6

350g/12oz shortcrust or sweet shortcrust
    pastry
3 firm pears
lemon juice
15ml/1 tbsp peach brandy or water
60ml/4 tbsp peach preserve, strained

For the almond cream filling
115g/4oz/¾ cup blanched whole almonds
50g/2oz/¼ cup caster sugar
65g/2½oz/5 tbsp butter
1 egg, plus 1 egg white
few drops almond essence

1 Roll out the pastry thinly and use to line a 23cm/9in flan tin. Chill the pastry case while you make the filling. Put the almonds and sugar in a food processor and pulse until finely ground; they should not be paste. Add the butter and process until creamy, then add the egg, egg white and almond essence and mix well.

2 Place a baking sheet in the oven and preheat to 190°C/375°F/Gas 5. Peel the pears, halve them, remove the cores and rub with lemon juice.

3 Put the pear halves cut-side down on a board and slice thinly crossways, keeping the slices together.

4 Pour the almond cream filling into the pastry case. Slide a palette knife under one pear half and press the top with your fingers to fan out the slices. Transfer to the tart, placing the fruit on the filling like spokes of a wheel. If you like, remove a few slices from each half before arranging and use to fill in any gaps in the centre.

5 Place on the baking sheet and bake for 50–55 minutes until the filling is set and well browned. Cool on a rack.

6 Meanwhile, heat the brandy or water and the preserve in a small saucepan, then brush over the top of the hot tart to glaze. Serve the tart warm, at room temperature.

Sachertorte

This glorious gâteau was created in Vienna in 1832 by Franz Sacher, a chef in the royal household.

INGREDIENTS

Serves 10–12

225g/8oz plain dark chocolate, broken into squares

150g/5oz/⅔ cup unsalted butter, softened

115g/4oz/generous ½ cup caster sugar

8 eggs, separated

115g/4oz/1 cup plain flour

For the glaze

225g/8oz/scant 1 cup apricot jam

15ml/1 tbsp lemon juice

For the icing

225g/8oz plain dark chocolate, broken into squares

200g/7oz/1 cup caster sugar

15ml/1 tbsp golden syrup

250ml/8fl oz/1 cup double cream

5ml/1 tsp vanilla essence

plain chocolate curls, to decorate

1 Preheat the oven to 180°C/350°F/Gas 4. Grease a 23cm/9in round springform cake tin and line with non-stick baking paper. Melt the chocolate in a heatproof bowl over hot water, then remove from the heat.

2 Cream the butter with the sugar in a mixing bowl until pale and fluffy, then add the egg yolks, one at a time, beating after each addition. Beat in the melted chocolate, then sift the flour over the mixture and fold it in evenly.

3 Whisk the egg whites in a clean, grease-free bowl until stiff, then stir about a quarter of the whites into the chocolate mixture to lighten it. Fold in the remaining whites.

4 Tip the mixture into the prepared cake tin and smooth level. Bake for about 50–55 minutes, or until firm. Turn out carefully on to a wire rack to cool.

5 Heat the apricot jam with the lemon juice in a small saucepan until melted, then strain through a sieve into a bowl. Once the cake is cold, slice in half across the middle to make two equal-size layers.

6 Brush the top and sides of each layer with the apricot glaze, then sandwich them together. Place on a wire rack.

7 Mix the icing ingredients in a heavy saucepan. Heat gently, stirring until thick. Simmer for 3–4 minutes, without stirring, until the mixture registers 95°C/200°F on a sugar thermometer. Pour quickly over the cake and spread evenly. Leave to set, then decorate with chocolate curls.

Chocolate Soufflés

These are easy to make and can be prepared in advance – the filled dishes can wait for up to one hour before baking. For best results, use good quality Continental chocolate.

INGREDIENTS

Serves 6

175g/6oz plain chocolate, chopped

150g/5oz/⅔ cup unsalted butter, cut in small pieces

4 large eggs, separated

30ml/2 tbsp orange liqueur (optional)

1.5ml/¼ tsp cream of tartar

45ml/3 tbsp caster sugar

icing sugar, for dusting

sprigs of redcurrants and white chocolate roses, to decorate

For the white chocolate sauce

75g/3oz white chocolate, chopped

90ml/6 tbsp whipping cream

15–30ml/1–2 tbsp orange liqueur

grated rind of ½ orange

1 Generously butter six 150ml/ ¼ pint/⅓ cup ramekins. Sprinkle each with a little caster sugar and tap out any excess. Place the ramekins on a baking sheet.

2 In a heavy saucepan over a very low heat, melt the chocolate and butter, stirring until smooth. Remove from the heat and cool slightly, then beat in the egg yolks and orange liqueur, if using. Set aside, stirring occasionally.

3 Preheat the oven to 220°C/ 425°F/Gas 7. In a clean, grease-free bowl, whisk the egg whites slowly until frothy. Add the cream of tartar, increase the spreed and whisk until they form soft peaks. Gradually sprinkle over the sugar, 15ml/1 tbsp at a time, whisking until the whites are stiff and glossy.

4 Stir a third of the whites into the cooled chocolate mixture to lighten it, then pour the chocolate mixture over the remaining whites. Using a rubber spatula or large metal spoon, gently fold the sauce into the whites. (Don't worry about a few white streaks.) Spoon into the prepared dishes.

5 To make the white chocolate sauce, put the chopped white chocolate and the cream into a small saucepan. Place over a low heat and cook, stirring constantly until melted and smooth. Remove from the heat and stir in the liqueur and orange rind, then pour into a serving jug and keep warm.

6 Bake the soufflés for 10–12 minutes until risen and set, but still slightly wobbly in the centre. Dust with icing sugar and decorate with a sprig of redcurrants and a white chocolate rose. Serve the sauce separately.

Bitter Chocolate Mousse

This is the quintessential French dessert – easy to prepare ahead, rich and extremely delicious. Use the darkest chocolate you can find for the most authentic and intense chocolate flavour.

INGREDIENTS

Serves 8

225g/8oz plain chocolate, chopped
30ml/2 tbsp orange liqueur or brandy
25g/1oz/2 tbsp unsalted butter, cut into
   small pieces
4 eggs, separated
90ml/6 tbsp whipping cream
1.5ml/¼ tsp cream of tartar
45ml/3 tbsp caster sugar
crème fraîche or soured cream and
   chocolate curls, to decorate

1 Place the chocolate and 60ml/ 4 tbsp of water in a heavy saucepan. Melt over a low heat, stirring until smooth. Remove the pan from the heat and whisk in the liqueur and butter.

2 With an electric mixer, beat the egg yolks for 2–3 minutes until thick and creamy, then slowly beat into the melted chocolate until well blended. Set aside.

3 Whip the cream until soft peaks form and stir a spoonful into the chocolate to lighten it. Fold in the remaining cream.

4 In a clean, grease-free bowl, using an electric mixer, beat the egg whites until frothy. Add the cream of tartar and continue beating until they form soft peaks. Gradually sprinkle over the sugar and continue beating until the whites are stiff and glossy.

5 Using a rubber spatula or large metal spoon, stir quarter of the egg whites into the chocolate mixture, then gently fold in the remaining whites, cutting down to the bottom, along the sides and up to the top in a semicircular motion until they are just combined. (Don't worry about a few white streaks.) Gently spoon into a 2 litre/3½ pint/8 cup dish or into eight individual dishes. Chill for at least 2 hours until set and chilled.

6 Spoon a little crème fraîche or soured cream over the mousse and decorate with chocolate curls.

Mocha Cream Pots

The name of this rich baked custard, a classic French dessert, comes from the baking cups, called pots de crème. *The addition of coffee gives the dessert an exotic touch.*

Serves 8

15ml/1 tbsp instant coffee powder
475ml/16fl oz/2 cups milk
75g/3oz/⅓ cup caster sugar
225g/8oz plain chocolate, chopped
10ml/2 tsp vanilla essence
30ml/2 tbsp coffee liqueur (optional)
7 egg yolks
whipped cream and crystallized mimosa
   balls, to decorate (optional)

1 Preheat the oven to 160°C/325°F/Gas 3. Place eight 120ml/4fl oz/½ cup *pots de crème* cups or ramekins in a roasting tin.

2 Put the instant coffee into a saucepan and stir in the milk, then add the sugar and set the pan over a medium-high heat. Bring to the boil, stirring constantly, until the coffee and sugar have dissolved.

3 Remove the pan from the heat and add the chocolate. Stir until the chocolate has melted and the sauce is smooth. Stir in the vanilla essence and coffee liqueur, if using.

4 In a bowl, whisk the egg yolks to blend them lightly. Slowly whisk in the chocolate mixture until well blended, then strain the mixture into a large jug and divide equally among the cups or ramekins. Place them in a roasting tin and pour in enough boiling water to come halfway up the sides of the cups or ramekins. Cover tin with foil.

5 Bake for 30–35 minutes until the custard is just set and a knife inserted into a custard comes out clean. Remove the cups or ramekins from the roasting tin and allow to cool. Place on a baking sheet, cover and chill completely. Decorate with the whipped cream and crystallized mimosa balls, if using.

Tiramisù

"Tiramisù" is Italian for "pick me up", and this rich egg and coffee dessert does just that!

INGREDIENTS

Serves 6–8

500g/1¼lb mascarpone cheese

5 eggs, separated, at room temperature

90g/3½oz/½ cup caster sugar

pinch of salt

savoyard or sponge biscuits, to line dish(es)

120ml/4fl oz/½ cup strong espresso coffee

60ml/4 tbsp brandy or rum (optional)

unsweetened cocoa powder, to sprinkle

1 Beat the mascarpone in a small bowl until soft. In a separate bowl beat the egg yolks with the sugar (reserving 15ml/1 tbsp) until the mixture is pale yellow and fluffy. Gradually beat in the softened mascarpone.

2 Using an electric beater or wire whisk, beat the egg whites with the salt until they form stiff peaks. Fold the egg whites into the mascarpone mixture.

3 Line one large or 6–8 individual serving dishes with the biscuits. Add the reserved sugar to the coffee, and stir in the liqueur, if using.

4 Sprinkle the coffee over the biscuits. They should be moist but not saturated. Cover with half of the egg mixture. Make another layer of biscuits moistened with coffee, and cover with the remaining egg mixture. Sprinkle with cocoa powder. Chill for at least 1 hour, preferably more, before serving.

Zabaglione

This Italian airy egg custard fortified with sweet wine is usually eaten warm with biscuits or fruit.

INGREDIENTS

Serves 3–4

3 egg yolks

45ml/3 tbsp caster sugar

75ml/5 tbsp marsala or white dessert wine

pinch of grated orange rind

1 In the top half of a double boiler, or in a heatproof bowl, away from the heat, whisk the egg yolks with the sugar until pale yellow. Beat in the marsala or white dessert wine.

2 Place the pan or bowl over a pan of simmering water, and continue whisking until the custard is a frothy, light mass and evenly coats the back of a spoon, 6–8 minutes. Do not let the upper container touch the hot water, or the zabaglione may curdle.

3 Stir in the orange rind. Serve immediately.

COOK'S TIP

A small teaspoon of ground cinnamon may be added.

Chocolate Profiteroles

This mouth-watering dessert is served in cafés throughout France. Sometimes the profiteroles are filled with whipped cream instead of ice cream, but they are always drizzled with chocolate sauce.

Serves 4–6

275g/10oz plain chocolate
750ml/1¼ pints/3 cups vanilla ice cream

For the profiteroles
110g/3¾oz/¾ cup plain flour
1.5ml/¼ tsp salt
pinch of freshly grated nutmeg
75g/3oz/6 tbsp unsalted butter, cut into 6 pieces
3 eggs

1 Preheat the oven to 200°C/400°F/Gas 6 and butter a baking sheet.

2 To make the profiteroles, sift together the flour, salt and nutmeg. In a medium saucepan, bring the butter and 175ml/6fl oz/¾ cup of water to the boil. Remove from the heat and add the dry ingredients all at once. Beat with a wooden spoon for about 1 minute until well blended and the mixture starts to pull away from the sides of the pan, then set the pan over a low heat and cook the mixture for about 2 minutes, beating constantly. Remove from the heat.

3 Beat one egg in a small bowl and set aside. Add the remaining eggs, one at a time, to the flour mixture, beating well. Add the beaten egg gradually until the dough is smooth and shiny; it should fall slowly when dropped from a spoon.

4 Using a tablespoon, drop the dough on to the baking sheet in 12 mounds. Bake for 25–30 minutes until the pastry is well risen and browned. Turn off the oven and leave the puffs to cool with the oven door open.

5 To make the sauce, place the chocolate and 120ml/4fl oz/½ cup of warm water in a double boiler or in a bowl over a pan of hot water and melt, stirring occasionally.

6 Split the profiteroles in half and put a small scoop of ice cream in each. Arrange on a serving platter. Pour the sauce over the top and serve at once.

Tarte Tatin

*This upside-down apple tart was
first made by two sisters who served
it in their restaurant in the Loire
Valley in France.*

Serves 8–10

225g/8oz puff or shortcrust pastry
10–12 large Golden Delicious apples
lemon juice
115g/4oz/½ cup butter, cut into pieces
90g/3½oz/½ cup caster sugar
1.5ml/½ tsp ground cinnamon
crème fraîche or whipped cream, to serve

1 On a lightly floured surface, roll
out the pastry into a 28cm/11in
round less than 5mm/¼in thick.
Transfer to a lightly floured baking
sheet and chill.

2 Peel the apples, cut them in half
lengthwise and core. Sprinkle
them generously with lemon juice.

3 Preheat the oven to
230°C/450°F/Gas 8. In a
25cm/10in tarte tatin tin, cook the
butter, sugar and cinnamon over
medium heat until the butter has
melted and sugar dissolved,
stirring occasionally. Continue
cooking for 6–8 minutes, until the
mixture turns a medium caramel
colour, then remove the pan from
the heat and arrange the apple
halves, standing on their edges, in
the tin, fitting them in tightly since
they shrink during cooking.

4 Return the apple-filled tin
to the heat and bring to a
simmer over a medium heat for
20–25 minutes until the apples are
tender and coloured. Remove the
tin from the heat and cool slightly.

5 Place the pastry on top of the
apple-filled pan and tuck the
edges of the pastry inside the edge
of the tin around the apples.

6 Pierce the pastry in two or
three places, then bake for
25–30 minutes until the pastry is
golden and the filling is bubbling.
Let the tart cool in the tin for
10–15 minutes.

7 To serve, run a sharp knife
around the edge of the tin to
loosen the pastry. Cover with a
serving plate and, holding them
tightly, carefully invert the tin and
plate together (do this over the
sink in case any caramel drips).
Lift off the tin and loosen any
apples that stick with a spatula.
Serve the tart warm with cream.

Greek Chocolate Mousse Tartlets

The combination of white chocolate and Greek-style yogurt makes an irresistibly light, but not too sweet, filling.

INGREDIENTS

Serves 6

175g/6oz/1½ cups plain flour
30ml/2 tbsp cocoa powder
30ml/2 tbsp icing sugar
115g/4oz/½ cup butter
melted dark chocolate, to decorate

For the filling

200g/7oz white chocolate, broken into squares
120ml/4fl oz/½ cup milk
10ml/2 tsp powdered gelatine
30ml/2 tbsp caster sugar
5ml/1 tsp vanilla essence
2 eggs, separated
250g/9oz/generous 1 cup Greek-style yogurt

1 Preheat the oven to 190°C/375°F/Gas 5. Sift the flour, cocoa and icing sugar into a large bowl.

2 Place the butter in a pan with 60ml/4 tbsp water and heat gently until just melted. Cool, then stir into the flour to make a smooth dough. Chill until firm.

3 Roll out the pastry and line six deep 10cm/4in loose-based flan tins.

4 Prick the base of each pastry case all over with a fork, cover with greaseproof paper weighed down with baking beans and bake blind for 10 minutes. Remove the baking beans and paper, return to the oven and bake a further 15 minutes, or until the pastry is firm. Leave to cool in the tins.

5 Make the filling. Melt the chocolate in a heatproof bowl over hot water. Pour the milk into a saucepan, sprinkle over the gelatine and heat gently, stirring, until the gelatine has dissolved completely. Remove from the heat and stir in the chocolate.

6 Whisk the sugar, vanilla essence and egg yolks in a large bowl, then beat in the chocolate mixture. Beat in the yogurt until evenly mixed.

7 Whisk the egg whites in a clean, grease-free bowl until stiff, then fold into the mixture. Divide among the pastry cases and leave to set.

8 Drizzle the melted white chocolate over the tartlets to decorate.

Chestnut Pudding

This is an Italian speciality, made during the months of October and November, when fresh sweet chestnuts are gathered.

Serves 4–5

450g/1lb fresh sweet chestnuts

300ml/½ pint/1¼ cups milk

115g/4oz/½ cup caster sugar

2 eggs, separated, at room temperature

25g/1oz/¼ cup unsweetened
   cocoa powder

2.5ml/½ tsp pure vanilla essence

50g/2oz/½ cup icing sugar, sifted

fresh whipped cream, to garnish

marrons glacés, to garnish

1 Cut a cross in the side of the chestnuts, and drop them into a pan of boiling water. Cook for 5–6 minutes. Remove with a slotted spoon, and peel while still warm.

2 Place the peeled chestnuts in a heavy or non-stick saucepan with the milk and half of the caster sugar. Cook over low heat, stirring occasionally, until soft. Remove from the heat and allow to cool. Press the contents of the pan through a strainer.

3 Preheat the oven to 180°C/ 350°F/Gas 4. Beat the egg yolks with the remaining caster sugar until the mixture is pale yellow and fluffy. Beat in the cocoa powder and the vanilla.

4 In a separate bowl, whisk the egg whites with a wire whisk or electric beater until they form soft peaks. Gradually beat in the sifted icing sugar and continue beating until the mixture forms stiff peaks.

5 Fold the chestnut and egg yolk mixtures together. Fold in the egg whites. Turn the mixture into one large or several individual buttered pudding moulds. Place on a baking sheet, and bake in the oven for 12–20 minutes, depending on the size. Remove from the oven, and allow to cool for 10 minutes before unmoulding. Serve garnished with whipped cream and marrons glacés.

Coffee Granita

A granita is a cross between a frozen drink and a flavoured ice, very popular in Italy. The consistency should be slushy, not solid. They can be made at home with the help of a food processor.

INGREDIENTS

Serves 4–5

115g/4oz/½ cup granulated sugar

250ml/8fl oz/1 cup very strong espresso coffee, cooled

whipped cream, to garnish (optional)

1 Heat 475ml/16fl oz/2 cups of water with the sugar over low heat until the sugar dissolves. Bring to the boil. Remove from the heat and allow to cool.

2 Combine the coffee with the sugar syrup. Place in a shallow container or freezer tray, and freeze until solid. Plunge the bottom of the frozen container or tray in very hot water for a few seconds. Turn the frozen mixture out, and chop it into large chunks.

3 Place the mixture in a food processor fitted with a metal blade, and process until it forms small crystals. Spoon into serving glasses and top with whipped cream, if desired. If you do not wish to serve the granita immediately, pour the processed mixture back into a shallow container or ice tray and freeze until serving time. Allow to thaw for a few minutes before serving, or process again.

Lemon Granita

Nothing is more refreshing on a hot summer's day than a cooling lemon granita.

INGREDIENTS

Serves 4–5

115g/4oz/½ cup granulated sugar

grated rind of 1 lemon, scrubbed before grating

juice of 2 large lemons

1 Heat 475ml/16fl oz/2 cups of water with the sugar over low heat until the sugar dissolves. Bring to the boil. Remove from the heat, and allow to cool.

2 Combine the lemon rind and juice with the sugar syrup. Place in a shallow container or freezer tray, and freeze until solid.

3 Plunge the bottom of the frozen container or tray in very hot water for a few seconds. Turn the frozen mixture out, and chop it into chunks.

4 Place the mixture in a food processor fitted with a metal blade, and process until it forms small crystals. Spoon into individual serving glasses.

Peach Melba

The story goes that one of the great French chefs, Auguste Escoffier, created this dessert in honour of the opera singer Nellie Melba, now forever enshrined in culinary, if not musical, history.

INGREDIENTS

Serves 6

50g/2oz/¼ cup caster sugar
1 vanilla pod, split lengthways
3 large peaches

For the sauce
450g/1lb/2⅔ cups fresh or frozen
   raspberries
15ml/1 tbsp lemon juice
25–40g/1–1½oz/2–3 tbsp caster sugar
30–45ml/2–3 tbsp raspberry liqueur
   (optional)
vanilla ice cream, to serve
mint leaves and fresh raspberries, to
   decorate (optional)

1 In a saucepan large enough to hold the peach halves in a single layer, combine 1 litre/ 1¾ pints/4 cups of water with the sugar and vanilla pod. Bring to the boil over a medium heat, stirring occasionally to dissolve the sugar.

2 Cut the peaches in half and twist the halves to separate them. Using a small teaspoon, remove the peach stones. Add the peach halves to the poaching syrup, cut-sides down, adding more water, if needed, to cover the fruit. Press a piece of greaseproof paper against the surface, reduce the heat to medium-low, then cover and simmer for 12–15 minutes until tender – the time will depend on the ripeness of the fruit. Remove the pan from the heat and leave the peaches to cool in the syrup.

3 Remove the peaches from the syrup and peel off the skins. Place on several thicknesses of kitchen paper to drain (reserve the syrup for another use), then cover and chill.

4 Put the raspberries, lemon juice and sugar in a blender or food processor fitted with the metal blade. Process for 1 minute, scraping down the sides once. Press through a fine sieve into a small bowl, then stir in the raspberry liqueur, if using, and put in the fridge to chill.

5 To serve, place a peach half, cut-side up, on a dessert plate, fill with a scoop of vanilla ice cream and spoon the raspberry sauce over the ice cream. Decorate with mint leaves and a few fresh raspberries, if using.

Australian Hazelnut Pavlova

Meringue topped with fresh fruit and cream – perfect for summer dinner parties.

INGREDIENTS

Serves 4–6

3 egg whites

175g/6oz/generous ¾ cup caster sugar

5ml/1 tsp cornflour

5ml/1 tsp white wine vinegar

40g/1½oz/5 tbsp chopped roasted
    hazelnuts

250ml/8fl oz/1 cup double cream

15ml/1 tbsp orange juice

30ml/2 tbsp natural thick and creamy
    yogurt

2 ripe nectarines, stoned and sliced

225g/8oz/1⅓ cups raspberries

15–30ml/1–2 tbsp redcurrant jelly,
    warmed

1 Preheat the oven to 140°C/275°F/Gas 1. Lightly grease a baking sheet. Draw a 20cm/8in circle on a sheet of baking parchment. Place pencil-side down on the baking sheet.

2 Place the egg whites in a clean, grease-free bowl and whisk with an electric mixer until stiff. Whisk in the sugar 15ml/1 tbsp at a time, whisking well after each addition.

3 Add the cornflour, vinegar and hazelnuts and fold in carefully with a large metal spoon.

4 Spoon the meringue on to the marked circle and spread out, making a dip in the centre.

5 Bake for about 1¼–1½ hours, until crisp. Leave to cool, then transfer to a serving platter.

6 Whip the cream and orange juice until just thick, stir in the yogurt and spoon on to the meringue. Top with the fruit and drizzle over the redcurrant jelly. Serve immediately.

Lemon Ricotta Cake

This lemony cake from Sardinia is quite different from a traditional cheesecake.

INGREDIENTS

Serves 6–8

75g/3oz/6 tbsp butter

175g/6oz/¾ cup granulated sugar

75g/3oz/generous ⅓ cup ricotta cheese

3 eggs, separated

175g/6oz/1½ cups plain flour

grated rind of 1 lemon

45ml/3 tbsp fresh lemon juice

7.5ml/1½ tsp baking powder

icing sugar, for dusting

1 Grease a 23cm/9in round cake or springform tin. Line the bottom with baking parchment or greaseproof paper. Grease the paper. Dust with flour. Set aside. Preheat the oven to 180°C/350°F/Gas 4.

2 Cream the butter and sugar together until smooth. Beat in the ricotta cheese.

3 Beat in the egg yolks, one at a time. Add 30ml/2 tbsp of the flour, and the lemon rind and juice. Sift the baking powder into the remaining flour and beat into the batter until well blended only.

4 Beat the egg whites until they form stiff peaks. Fold them carefully into the batter.

5 Turn the mixture into the prepared tin. Bake for 45 minutes, or until a cake tester inserted in the centre of the cake comes out clean. Allow the cake to cool for 10 minutes before turning it out on to a rack to cool. Dust the cake generously with icing sugar before serving.

Peaches with Amaretti Stuffing

Peaches are plentiful all over Italy. They are sometimes prepared hot, as in this classic dish.

INGREDIENTS

Serves 4

4 ripe fresh peaches

juice of ½ lemon

65g/2½oz/⅔ cup amaretti biscuits, crushed

30ml/2 tbsp marsala, brandy or peach brandy

25g/1oz/2 tbsp butter, at room temperature

2.5ml/½ tsp vanilla essence

30ml/2 tbsp granulated sugar

1 egg yolk

1 Preheat the oven to 180°C/350°F/Gas 4. Wash the peaches. Cut them in half and remove the stones. Enlarge the hollow left by the stones by scooping out some of the peach with a small spoon. Sprinkle the peach halves with the lemon juice.

2 Soften the amaretti crumbs in the marsala or brandy for a few minutes. Beat the butter until soft. Stir in the amaretti mixture and all the remaining ingredients.

3 Arrange the peach halves in a baking dish in one layer hollow side upwards. Divide the amaretti mixture into 8 parts, and fill the hollows, mounding the stuffing up in the centre. Bake for 35–40 minutes. These are delicious served hot or cold.

Bread Pudding with Pecan Nuts

A version of the British classic deliciously flavoured with pecan nuts and orange rind.

INGREDIENTS

Serves 6

400ml/14fl oz/1⅔ cups milk

400ml/14fl oz/1⅔ cups single or whipping
   cream

150g/5oz/¾ cup caster sugar

3 eggs, beaten to mix

10ml/2 tsp grated orange rind

5ml/1 tsp vanilla essence

24 slices of day-old French bread,
   1.5cm/½in thick

75g/3oz/½ cup toasted pecan nuts,
   chopped

icing sugar, for sprinkling

whipped cream or soured cream and
   maple syrup, to serve

1 Put 350ml/12fl oz/1½ cups each of the milk and cream in a saucepan. Add the sugar. Warm over low heat, stirring to dissolve the sugar. Remove from the heat and cool. Add the eggs, orange rind and vanilla and mix well.

2 Arrange half of the bread slices in a buttered 23–25cm/9–10in baking dish. Scatter two-thirds of the pecans over the bread. Arrange the remaining bread slices on top and scatter on the rest of the pecans.

3 Pour the egg mixture evenly over the bread slices. Soak for 30 minutes. Press the top layer of bread down into the liquid once or twice.

4 Preheat the oven to 180°C/350°F/Gas 4. If the top layer of bread slices looks dry and all the liquid has been absorbed, moisten with the remaining milk and cream.

5 Set the baking dish in a roasting tin. Add enough water to the tin to come halfway up the sides of the dish. Bring the water to the boil.

6 Transfer to the oven. Bake for 40 minutes or until the pudding is set and golden brown on top. Sprinkle the top of the pudding with sifted icing sugar and serve warm, with whipped cream or soured cream and maple syrup, if you like.

Spiced Peach Crumble

The topping of this classic dessert has rolled oats added for extra crunchiness.

INGREDIENTS

Serves 6

1.5kg/3lb ripe but firm peaches, peeled, stoned and sliced
60ml/4 tbsp caster sugar
2.5ml/½ tsp ground cinnamon
5ml/1 tsp lemon juice
whipped cream or vanilla ice cream, for serving (optional)

For the topping
115g/4oz/1 cup plain flour
1.5ml/¼ tsp ground cinnamon
1.5ml/¼ tsp ground allspice
75g/3oz/1 cup rolled oats
175g/6oz/¾ cup soft light brown sugar
115g/4oz/8 tbsp butter

1 Preheat the oven to 190°C/375°F/Gas 5. For the topping, sift the flour and spices into a bowl. Add the oats and sugar and stir to combine. Cut or rub in the butter until the mixture resembles coarse crumbs.

2 Toss the peaches with the sugar, cinnamon and lemon juice. Put the fruit mixture in a 20–23cm/8–9in diameter baking dish.

3 Scatter the topping over the fruit in an even layer. Bake for 30–35 minutes. Serve warm, with whipped cream or vanilla ice cream, if liked.

VARIATION

Use apricots or nectarines instead of peaches. Substitute nutmeg for the cinnamon.

Jam Tart

Jam tarts are popular in Italy where they are traditionally decorated with pastry strips.

Serves 6–8

200g/7oz/1¾ cups plain flour

pinch of salt

50g/2oz/¼ cup granulated sugar

115g/4oz/½ cup butter or margarine, chilled

1 egg

1.5ml/¼ tsp grated lemon rind

350g/12oz/1¼ cups fruit jam, such as raspberry, apricot or strawberry

1 egg, lightly beaten with 30ml/2 tbsp whipping cream, for glazing

1 Make the pastry by placing the flour, salt and sugar in a mixing bowl. Using a pastry blender or two knives, cut the butter or margarine into the dry ingredients as quickly as possible until the mixture resembles coarse crumbs.

2 Beat the egg with the lemon rind in a cup, and pour it over the flour mixture. Combine with a fork until the dough holds together. If it is too crumbly, mix in 15–30ml/1–2 tbsp of water.

3 Gather the dough into two balls, one slightly larger than the other, and flatten into discs. Wrap in greaseproof or waxed paper, and put in the fridge for at least 40 minutes.

4 Lightly grease a shallow 23cm/9in tart or pie tin, preferably with a removable bottom. Roll out the larger disc of pastry on a lightly floured surface to a thickness of about 3mm/⅛in.

5 Roll the pastry around the rolling pin and transfer to the prepared tin. Trim the edges evenly with a small knife. Prick the bottom with a fork. Chill for at least 30 minutes.

6 Preheat the oven to 190°C/375°F/Gas 5. Spread the jam thickly and evenly over the base of the pastry. Roll out the remaining pastry.

7 Cut the pastry into strips about 1cm/¼in wide using a ruler as a guide. Arrange them over the jam in a lattice pattern. Trim the edges of the strips even with the edge of the tin, pressing them lightly on to the pastry shell. Brush the pastry with the egg and cream glaze. Bake for about 35 minutes, or until the pastry is golden brown. Allow to cool before serving.

Indian Ice Cream (Kulfi)

Kulfi-wallahs (ice cream vendors) have always made kulfi, and continue to this day, without using modern freezers. Try this method – it works extremely well in an ordinary freezer. You will need to start making kulfi the day before you want to serve it.

INGREDIENTS

Serves 4–6

3 x 400ml/14fl oz cans evaporated milk

3 egg whites, whisked until peaks form

350g/12oz/3 cups icing sugar

5ml/1 tsp cardamom powder

15ml/1 tbsp rose water

175g/6oz/1½ cups pistachios, chopped

75g/3oz/generous ½ cup sultanas

75g/3oz/¾ cup sliced almonds

25g/1oz/2 tbsp glacé cherries, halved

1 Remove the labels from the cans of evaporated milk and lay the cans down in a pan with a tight-fitting cover. Fill the pan with water to reach three-quarters up the cans. Bring to the boil, cover and simmer for 20 minutes. When cool, remove and chill the cans in the fridge for 24 hours.

2 Open the cans and empty the milk into a large, chilled bowl. Whisk until it doubles in quantity, then fold in the whisked egg whites and icing sugar.

3 Gently fold in the remaining ingredients, seal the bowl with cling film and leave in the freezer for 1 hour.

4 Remove the ice cream from the freezer and mix well with a fork. Transfer to a freezer container and return to the freezer for a final setting. Remove from the freezer 10 minutes before serving in scoops.

Spiced Mexican Fritters

Hot, sweet and spicy fritters are popular in both Spain and Mexico for either breakfast or a snack.

INGREDIENTS

Makes 16 (serves 4)
175g/6oz/1 cup raspberries
45ml/3 tbsp icing sugar
45ml/3 tbsp orange juice

For the fritters
50g/2oz/4 tbsp butter
65g/2½oz/⅔ cup plain flour, sifted
2 eggs, lightly beaten
15ml/1 tbsp ground almonds
corn oil, for frying
15ml/1 tbsp icing sugar and 2.5ml/½ tsp
   ground cinnamon, for dusting
8 fresh raspberries, to decorate

1 Mash the raspberries with the icing sugar, push through a sieve into a bowl to remove all the seeds. Stir in the orange juice and chill until ready to serve.

2 To make the fritters, place the butter and 150ml/¼ pint/ ⅔ cup water in a saucepan and heat gently until the butter has melted. Bring to the boil and, when boiling, add the sifted flour all at once and turn off the heat.

3 Beat until the mixture leaves the sides of the pan and forms a ball. Cool slightly then beat in the eggs a little at a time, then add the almonds.

4 Spoon the mixture into a piping bag fitted with a large star nozzle. Half-fill a saucepan or deep-fat fryer with the oil and heat to 190°C/375°F.

5 Pipe about four 5cm/2in lengths at a time into the hot oil, cutting off the raw mixture with a knife as you go. Deep-fry for about 3–4 minutes, turning occasionally, until puffed up and golden. Drain on kitchen paper and keep warm in the oven while frying the remainder.

6 When you have fried all the mixture, dust the hot fritters with icing sugar and cinnamon. Serve three or four per person on serving plates drizzled with a little of the raspberry sauce, dust again with sieved icing sugar and decorate with fresh raspberries.

Thai Fried Bananas

A very simple and quick Thai pudding – bananas fried in butter, brown sugar and lime juice, and sprinkled with toasted coconut.

INGREDIENTS

Serves 4
40g/1½oz/3 tbsp butter
4 large slightly under-ripe bananas
15ml/1 tbsp desiccated coconut
60ml/4 tbsp soft light brown sugar
60ml/4 tbsp lime juice
2 fresh lime slices, to decorate
thick and creamy natural yogurt, to serve

1 Heat the butter in a large frying pan or wok and fry the bananas for 1–2 minutes on each side, or until they are lightly golden in colour.

2 Meanwhile, dry-fry the coconut in a small frying pan until lightly browned, and reserve.

3 Sprinkle the sugar into the pan with the bananas, add the lime juice and cook, stirring until dissolved. Arrange bananas on a serving dish. Sprinkle the coconut over the bananas, decorate with lime slices and serve with the thick and creamy yogurt.

Index

Almonds: Bakewell tart, 211
chocolate almond meringue pie, 80
peach tart with almond cream, 200
pear and almond cream tart, 231
Amaretti: chocolate amaretti
peaches, 149
peaches with amaretti stuffing, 246
Amaretto soufflé, 58
Apples: apple brown Betty, 216
apple couscous pudding, 69
apple-cranberry lattice pie, 195
apple foam with blackberries, 116
apple fritters, 146
apple pie, 214
apple soufflé omelette, 162
apple strudel, 224
autumn pudding, 154
baked apples with apricot filling, 64
baked apples with caramel sauce, 62
emerald fruit salad, 94
Eve's pudding, 70
ruby fruit salad, 152
steamed chocolate and fruit
puddings, 78
tarte tatin, 239
Apricots: apricot and orange jelly, 22
apricot and orange roulade, 128
apricot and pear filo roulade, 158
apricots in Marsala, 136
apricots with orange cream, 30
baked apples with apricot filling, 64
cinnamon and apricot soufflés, 107
glazed apricot sponge, 82
quick apricot blender whip, 93
three-fruits compote, 91
yogurt with apricots and
pistachios, 88

Bakewell tart, 211
Bananas: almost instant banana
pudding, 98
banana and passion fruit whip, 106
banana ginger parkin, 133
banana honey yogurt ice, 154
banana orange loaf, 132
Boston banoffee pie, 221
Brazilian coffee bananas, 103
chocolate chip and banana
pudding, 81
fluffy banana and pineapple
mousse, 125
hot bananas with rum and
raisins, 139
hot fruit with maple butter, 150
ruby fruit salad, 152
Thai fried bananas, 252
Batter: hot plum batter pudding, 82
Blackberries: apple foam with blackberries, 116
autumn pudding, 154
blackberry cobbler, 163
lemon soufflé with blackberries, 25
rich chocolate-berry tart, 210
Blackcurrants: blackcurrant sorbet, 50
Russian fruit compote, 164

Blueberries: blueberry-hazelnut
cheesecake, 206
blueberry pancakes, 140
peach and blueberry pie, 186
Boodles orange fool, 22
Brandy butter, 18
Bread pudding with pecan nuts, 248
Butterscotch sauce, 18

Cabinet pudding, 70

Cakes: angel food cake, 176
banana ginger parkin, 133
banana orange loaf, 132
black and white pound cake, 181
Black Forest gâteau, 175
carrot cake with maple butter
frosting, 180
chocolate and cherry polenta
cake, 177
chocolate layer cake, 170
chocolate mousse strawberry layer
cake, 182
death by chocolate, 183
devil's food cake with orange
frosting, 174
Greek honey and lemon cake, 126
hot chocolate cake, 79
lemon coconut layer cake, 178
lemon ricotta cake, 246
marbled Swiss roll, 171
pineapple upside-down cake, 185
Sachertorte, 232
simple chocolate cake, 184
spiced date and walnut cake, 131
sponge cake with fruit and cream, 172
warm lemon and syrup cake, 74
Caramel: baked apples with

caramel sauce, 62
Carrot cake with maple butter
frosting, 180
Cheese: apricots with orange cream, 30
figs with ricotta cream, 90
fruity ricotta creams, 150
grilled nectarines with ricotta and
spice, 123
kiwi ricotta cheese tart, 203
lemon ricotta cake, 246

peach and ginger pashka, 94
tiramisù, 236
Cheesecake: blueberry-hazelnut
cheesecake, 206
chocolate cheesecake, 218
classic cheesecake, 218
raspberry and white chocolate
cheesecake, 208
Cherries: Black Forest gâteau, 175
cherries jubilee, 136
cherry compote, 146
cherry pancakes, 114
cherry pie, 192
cherry syllabub, 32
chocolate and cherry polenta cake, 177
Chestnuts: chestnut pudding, 241
chocolate and chestnut pots, 41
Chocolate: bitter chocolate mousse, 234
black and white pound cake, 181
Black Forest gâteau, 175
chocolate almond meringue pie, 80
chocolate amaretti peaches, 149
chocolate and cherry polenta cake, 177
chocolate and chestnut pots, 41
chocolate and orange Scotch
pancakes, 57
chocolate and orange soufflé, 66

chocolate cheesecake, 218
chocolate chiffon pie, 198
chocolate chip and banana
pudding, 81
chocolate crêpes with plums and
port, 72
chocolate fruit fondue, 224
chocolate fudge sauce, 19
chocolate fudge sundaes, 102
chocolate hazelnut galettes, 40
chocolate ice cream, 51
chocolate layer cake, 170
chocolate mandarin trifle, 26
chocolate mousse strawberry layer
cake, 182
chocolate pear tart, 205
chocolate pecan pie, 189
chocolate profiteroles, 238
chocolate soufflé crêpes, 73
chocolate soufflés, 233
chocolate vanilla timbales, 124
coffee, vanilla and chocolate stripe, 38
death by chocolate, 183
double chocolate snowball, 53
glossy chocolate sauce, 19
Greek chocolate mousse tartlets, 240
hot chocolate cake, 79
hot chocolate zabaglione, 56
hot mocha rum soufflés, 59
iced praline torte, 48
magic chocolate mud pudding, 75
marbled Swiss roll, 171
mocha cream pots, 235
pears in chocolate fudge blankets, 65
raspberry and white chocolate
cheesecake, 208
rich chocolate-berry tart, 210
simple chocolate cake, 184
steamed chocolate and fruit
puddings, 78
white chocolate mousse with dark
sauce, 46
white chocolate parfait, 44
Choux pastry, 10
chocolate profiteroles, 238
Christmas pudding, 76
Cinnamon: cinnamon and apricot
soufflés, 107
clementines in cinnamon caramel, 148
mince pies with orange cinnamon
pastry, 194
tropical fruits in cinnamon syrup, 142
Coconut: coconut cream pie, 199
Creole ambrosia, 36
lemon coconut layer cake, 178
Coffee: Brazilian coffee bananas, 103
cappuccino coffee cups, 117
coffee granita, 242
coffee ice cream with caramelized
pecans, 42
coffee, vanilla and chocolate stripe, 38
hot mocha rum soufflés, 59
mocha cream pots, 235
tiramisù, 236
Compote: cherry compote, 146

Russian fruit compote, 164
spiced red fruit compote, 166
three-fruits compote, 91
warm autumn compote, 156
Coulis: redcurrant and raspberry
coulis, 16
Couscous: apple couscous pudding, 69
Cranberries: apple-cranberry lattice
pie, 195
steamed chocolate and fruit
puddings, 78
Crème Anglaise, 17
Crème brûlée, 227
ginger and orange crème brûlée, 98
orange yogurt brûlées, 104
Crème caramel, 223
Creole ambrosia, 36
Crêpes. *See* Pancakes and crêpes
Cumberland rum butter, 18
Custard: Vermont baked maple
custard, 222

Dates: spiced date and walnut cake,
131

Eggs: apple soufflé omelette, 162
floating islands, 226
floating islands in hot plum
sauce, 122
Elderflowers: gooseberry and elderflower cream, 29
Eve's pudding, 70

Figs: figs with ricotta cream, 90
Greek fig and honey pudding, 164
warm autumn compote, 156
Filo pastry: apricot and pear filo
roulade, 158
filo chiffon pie, 129
Floating islands, 226
floating islands in hot plum
sauce, 122
Fools: Boodles orange fool, 22
rhubarb and orange fool, 30
French flan pastry, 9
Fritters: apple fritters, 146
spiced Mexican fritters, 252
Fruit. *See also* Apples, etc
autumn pudding, 154
chocolate fruit fondue, 224
coring and stoning, 13, 14
cutting, 14, 15
emerald fruit salad, 94
frudités with honey dip, 86
fruited rice ring, 113
fruit kebabs with mango and yogurt
sauce, 142
fruit tartlets, 190
fruity ricotta creams, 150
hot fruit with maple butter, 150
peeling and trimming, 12, 13
red berry tart with lemon cream
filling, 159
ruby fruit salad, 152
Russian fruit compote, 164
seeding, 13, 14
spiced red fruit compote, 166
sponge cake with fruit and
cream, 172
summer fruit salad ice cream, 118
summer pudding, 153

three-fruits compote, 91
tofu berry "cheesecake", 120
tropical fruits in cinnamon
syrup, 142
Fudge: chocolate fudge sauce, 19
chocolate fudge sundaes, 102
pears in chocolate fudge blankets, 65

Gelatine, 16
Ginger: banana ginger parkin, 133
ginger and orange crème brûlée, 98
ginger baked pears, 160
gingerbread upside-down pudding, 60
peach and ginger pashka, 94
watermelon, ginger and grapefruit
salad, 87

Gooseberries: crunchy gooseberry
crumble, 130
gooseberry and elderflower
cream, 29
Grand Marnier: frozen Grand
Marnier soufflés, 52
Granitas: coffee granita, 242
lemon granita, 242
Grapefruit: watermelon, ginger and
grapefruit salad, 87
Hazelnuts: Australian hazelnut
pavlova, 245
blueberry-hazelnut cheesecake, 206
chocolate hazelnut galettes, 40
raspberry meringue gâteau, 34
Honey: banana honey yogurt ice, 154
frudités with honey dip, 86
Greek fig and honey pudding, 164
Greek honey and lemon cake, 126

Ice cream: banana honey yogurt
ice, 154
chocolate fudge sundaes, 102
chocolate ice cream, 51
coffee ice cream with caramelized
pecans, 42

Indian ice cream, 251
peach Melba, 244
summer fruit salad ice cream, 118

Jam tart, 250
Jelly: apricot and orange jelly, 22
fresh citrus jelly, 110
Junket: rose petal cream, 32

Kiwi fruit: emerald fruit salad, 94
fruit kebabs with mango and yogurt
sauce, 142
kiwi ricotta cheese tart, 203
Kulfi, 251

Lemons: fresh citrus jelly, 110

Greek honey and lemon cake, 126
lemon and orange tart, 204
lemon coconut layer cake, 178
lemon granita, 242
lemon meringue pie, 196
lemon ricotta cake, 246
lemon soufflé with blackberries, 25
red berry tart with lemon cream
filling, 159
tarte au citron, 230
warm lemon and syrup cake, 74
Limes: fresh citrus jelly, 110
Key lime pie, 190
lime sherbet, 28

Mango: fruit kebabs with mango and
yogurt sauce, 142
hot fruit with maple butter, 150
mango sorbet, 144
tropical fruits in cinnamon
syrup, 142
Melon. *See also* Watermelon
emerald fruit salad, 94
ruby fruit salad, 152
three-fruits compote, 91
Meringue: Australian hazelnut
pavlova, 245

chocolate almond meringue pie, 80
floating islands, 226
floating islands in hot
plum sauce, 122
lemon meringue pie, 196
queen of puddings, 68
raspberry meringue gâteau, 34
Mince pies with orange cinnamon
pastry, 194
Mousses: bitter chocolate
mousse, 234
fluffy banana and pineapple
mousse, 240
frozen strawberry mousse cake, 47
Greek chocolate mousse
tartlets, 240
ruby plum mousse, 156
white chocolate mousse with dark
sauce, 46
Muesli: raspberry muesli layer, 97

Nectarines: grilled nectarines with
ricotta and spice, 123

Oranges: apricot and orange jelly, 22
apricot and orange roulade, 128
apricots with orange cream, 30
banana orange loaf, 132
Boodles orange fool, 22
chocolate and orange Scotch
pancakes, 57
chocolate and orange soufflé, 66
chocolate mandarin trifle, 26
clementines in cinnamon
caramel, 148
Creole ambrosia, 36
crêpes Suzette, 228
devil's food cake with orange frosting, 174
fresh citrus jelly, 110
ginger and orange crème brûlée, 98
lemon and orange tart, 204
mandarins in orange flower
syrup, 111
orange yogurt brûlées, 104
prune and orange pots, 92
rhubarb and orange fool, 30
ruby fruit salad, 152
tangerine trifle, 24

Pancakes and crêpes: blueberry
pancakes, 140
cherry pancakes, 114
chocolate crêpes with plums and
port, 72
chocolate soufflé crêpes, 73
crêpes Suzette, 228
Parfait: white chocolate parfait, 44
Passion fruit: banana and passion
fruit whip, 106
raspberry and passion fruit swirls, 96
Pastry: choux, 10
edge, finishing, 11
French flan, 9
pies. *See* Pies
rolling out, 11
shortcrust, 8
tarts and flans. *See* Tarts and flans
tin, lining, 11
tips for making, 8
Paw paws: hot fruit with maple
butter, 150

tropical fruits in cinnamon
syrup, 142
Peaches: chocolate amaretti
peaches, 149
gingerbread upside-down
pudding, 60
peach and blueberry pie, 186
peach and ginger pashka, 94
peach Melba, 244
peach cobbler, 61
peach tart with almond cream, 200
peaches with amaretti stuffing, 246
spiced peach crumble, 249
Pears: apricot and pear filo
roulade, 158
chocolate pear tart, 205
ginger baked pears, 160
pear and almond cream tart, 231
pears in chocolate fudge
blankets, 65
poached pears in red wine, 138
warm autumn compote, 156
warm lemon and syrup cake, 74
warm pears in cider, 100
Pecans: bread pudding with pecan
nuts, 248
chocolate pecan torte, 189
coffee ice cream with caramelized
pecans, 42
Mississippi pecan pie, 220
Pies: American spiced pumpkin
pie, 217
apple-cranberry lattice pie, 195
apple pie, 214
Boston banoffee pie, 221
cherry pie, 192
chocolate almond meringue pie, 80
chocolate chiffon pie, 198
coconut cream pie, 199
filo chiffon pie, 129
Key lime pie, 190
lemon meringue pie, 196
mince pies with orange cinnamon
pastry, 194
Mississippi pecan pie, 220
peach and blueberry pie, 186
rhubarb pie, 188
Pineapple: fluffy banana and
pineapple mousse, 125
fresh pineapple salad, 88
fruit kebabs with mango and yogurt
sauce, 142
grilled pineapple with rum
custard, 105
hot fruit with maple butter, 150
pineapple flambé, 100
pineapple upside-down cake, 185
three-fruits compote, 91
Pistachios: yogurt with apricots and
pistachios, 88
Plums: autumn pudding, 154
chocolate crêpes with plums and
port, 72
floating islands in hot plum
sauce, 122
hot plum batter pudding, 82
plum and port sorbet, 119
ruby plum mousse, 156
spiced red fruit compote, 166
Polenta: chocolate and cherry
polenta cake, 177

Praline: iced praline torte, 48
Prunes: prune and orange pots, 92
prunes poached in red wine, 160
Puddings: almost instant banana
pudding, 98
apple couscous pudding, 69
autumn pudding, 154
bread pudding with pecan nuts, 248
chestnut pudding, 241
chocolate chip and banana
pudding, 81
Christmas pudding, 76
Eve's pudding, 70
gingerbread upside-down
pudding, 60
glazed apricot sponge, 82

Greek fig and honey pudding, 164
hot plum batter pudding, 82
magic chocolate mud pudding, 75
queen of puddings, 68
steamed chocolate and fruit
puddings, 78
sticky toffee pudding, 66
summer pudding, 153
Pumpkin: American spiced pumpkin
pie, 217

Queen of puddings, 68

Raisins: hot bananas with rum and
raisins, 139
Raspberries: minted raspberry
bavarois, 112
raspberry and passion fruit
swirls, 96
raspberry and white chocolate
cheesecake, 208
raspberry meringue gâteau, 34
raspberry muesli layer, 97
raspberry tart, 202
raspberry trifle, 145
redcurrant and raspberry coulis, 16
rich chocolate-berry tart, 210

Russian fruit compote, 164
spiced Mexican fritters, 252
spiced red fruit compote, 166
warm autumn compote, 156
Redcurrants: redcurrant and
raspberry coulis, 16
Russian fruit compote, 164
Rhubarb: filo chiffon pie, 129
rhubarb and orange fool, 30
rhubarb pie, 188
rhubarb spiral cobbler, 166
rhubarb-strawberry crisp, 141
Rice: fruited rice ring, 113
Rose petal cream, 32
Roulade: apricot and orange
roulade, 128

apricot and pear filo roulade, 158
strawberry roulade, 126

Sabayon, 17
Sachertorte, 232
Sauces: butterscotch sauce, 18
caramel sauce, 62
chocolate fudge sauce, 19
crème Anglaise, 17
glossy chocolate sauce, 19
redcurrant and raspberry coulis, 16
sabayon, 17
Scotch pancakes: chocolate and
orange Scotch pancakes, 57
Semolina: chocolate and orange
soufflé, 66
Shortcrust pastry, 8
Sorbet: blackcurrant sorbet, 50
lime sherbet, 28
mango sorbet, 144
plum and port sorbet, 119
watermelon sherbet, 37
Soufflés: Amaretto soufflé, 58
apple soufflé omelette, 162
chocolate and orange soufflé, 66
chocolate soufflé crêpes, 73
chocolate soufflés, 233

cinnamon and apricot soufflés, 107
frozen Grand Marnier soufflés, 52
hot mocha rum soufflés, 59
lemon soufflé with blackberries, 25
Star fruit: emerald fruit salad, 94
tropical fruits in cinnamon
syrup, 142
Sticky toffee pudding, 66
Strawberries: chocolate mousse
strawberry layer cake, 182
frozen strawberry mousse cake, 47
fruit kebabs with mango and yogurt
sauce, 142
rhubarb-strawberry crisp, 141
spiced red fruit compote, 166
strawberry roulade, 126
Syllabub: cherry syllabub, 32

Tarts and flans: Bakewell tart, 211
chocolate pear tart, 205
fruit tartlets, 190
Greek chocolate mousse
tartlets, 240
jam tart, 250
kiwi ricotta cheese tart, 203
lemon and orange tart, 204
peach tart with almond cream, 200
pear and almond cream tart, 231
raspberry tart, 202
red berry tart with lemon cream
filling, 159
rich chocolate-berry tart, 210
tarte au citron, 230
tarte tatin, 239
treacle tart, 209
Tiramisù, 236
Toffee: sticky toffee pudding, 66
Tofu berry "cheesecake", 120
Torte: chocolate pecan torte, 189
iced praline torte, 48
Sachertorte, 232
Treacle tart, 209
Trifle: chocolate mandarin trifle, 26
raspberry trifle, 145
tangerine trifle, 24

Vanilla: chocolate vanilla
timbales, 124
coffee, vanilla and chocolate
stripe, 38

Walnuts: spiced date and walnut
cake, 131
Watermelon: watermelon sherbet, 37
watermelon, ginger and grapefruit
salad, 87

Yogurt: banana honey yogurt ice, 154
fruit kebabs with mango and yogurt
sauce, 142
Greek chocolate mousse
tartlets, 240
Greek fig and honey pudding, 164
orange yogurt brûlées, 104
quick apricot blender whip, 93
tofu berry "cheesecake", 120
yogurt with apricots and
pistachios, 88

Zabaglione, 236
hot chocolate zabaglione, 56

NOTES

NOTES

NOTES

NOTES

NOTES

NOTES